MW01118726

THE ALGER HISS COMMUNIST SPY TRIAL

A Headline Court Case

Headline Court Cases

THE ALGER HISS COMMUNIST SPY TRIAL

A Headline Court Case

Karen Alonso

Enslow Publishers, Inc.

40 Industrial Road   PO Box 38
Box 398   Aldershot
Berkeley Heights, NJ 07922 Hants GU12 6BP
USA   UK

http://www.enslow.com

Library of Congress Cataloging-in-Publication Data

Alonso, Karen.
  The Alger Hiss Communist spy trial : a headline court case / Karen Alonso.
    p. cm. – (Headline court cases)
  Includes bibliographical references and index.
  ISBN 0-7660-1483-5
  1. Hiss, Alger—Trials, litigation, etc.—Juvenile literature.
  2. Trials (Perjury)—New York (State)—New York—Juvenile literature.
  [1. Hiss, Alger—Trials, litigation, etc. 2. Trials (Perjury)] I. Title.
  II. Series.
  KF224.H57 A44 2001
  364.1'31—dc21
          00-010731

Printed in the United States of America

10 9 8 7 6 5 4 3   T 46898

To Our Readers:
We have done our best to make sure all Internet addresses in this book were active and
appropriate when we went to press. However, the author and the publisher have no con-
trol over and assume no liability for the material available on those Internet sites or on
other Web sites they may link to. Any comments or suggestions can be sent by e-mail to
comments@enslow.com or to the address on the back cover.

Photo Credits: © Bettmann/CORBIS, pp. 3, 8, 20, 25, 34, 36, 40, 42, 49, 51,
57, 59, 89, 100, 104; © CORBIS, p. 27; Library of Congress, *Dictionary of
American Portraits*, Dover Publications, Inc., © 1967, p. 18; Courtesy National
Security Agency, pp. 106, 108; © Hulton-Deutsch Collection/CORBIS, p. 73;
Library of Congress, pp. 10, 16; National Archives, p. 28; United States
Holocaust Memorial Museum, p. 32.

Cover Photo: © Bettmann/CORBIS

Contents

Introduction

In 1948, two men stood before the nation and made accusations that would capture America's attention. One, Whittaker Chambers, was an admitted ex-Communist spy. He claimed that the other man, Alger Hiss, had also been a Communist spy. Hiss was a well-respected man who had served his country in the State Department as an assistant secretary of state. He said that Chambers was a liar.

The clash between Chambers and Hiss became a symbol of a much larger conflict between the United States and the Soviet Union. This dispute was called the Cold War. Americans feared the potential for an actual war between the United States and the Soviet Union would become a reality. But the tension between the two countries never reached the level of actual combat.

There were many reasons for the conflict between the United States and the Soviet Union. One reason was the different types of societies represented by the two countries. The United States enjoys an open society. In this type of society, citizens enjoy the right to free speech and the free exchange of opinions and information. American citizens are able to travel from one state to another without having to inform the authorities.

The Soviet Union, on the other hand, was an example of what is known as a "closed society." Citizens of the Soviet

Whittaker Chambers (at microphone in front) testifies at the trial of Alger Hiss. Hiss (back row left, with white handkerchief in pocket) listens to his accuser. Newspaper and radio reporters surround the two men.

Union were not free to openly voice opinions. Soviets were also not free to travel either outside or within the Soviet Union without special permission from the government.

America's Suspicious Ally

America had an uneasy relationship with the Soviet Union. Since the 1917 Russian Revolution, the Soviet Union had operated under a system of communism. Under communism, all members of a society are expected to work and contribute to the good of the country. Each citizen shares in all the work and, theoretically, is entitled to share all the goods that are produced in that society.

This is a striking contrast to the system in effect in the

United States. America operates under a system called capitalism. Under capitalism, Americans pursue their own livelihoods and are free to enjoy the fruits of their own labors. Therefore, the United States and the Soviet Union not only differed in their form of government, or their economic system, but also had very real differences in philosophy.

These differences made for a very uncomfortable relationship between the two nations. Aside from these technical differences, many Americans were deeply opposed to the philosophy and goals of communism. In their effort to create a world in which all nations would recognize and utilize the system of communism, Communists believed that any means should be used to achieve their goal. Karl Marx, author of the *Communist Manifesto*, claimed that there should be no such thing as private property. Furthermore, Marx wrote that the right to inherit wealth should be abolished.

The most troubling aspect of communism for many Americans was the idea proposed by Karl Marx that capitalist societies should be eliminated. According to Marx, the goals of communism could be "attained only by the forcible overthrow of all existing social conditions."[1] Since all of society is the history of struggles between the classes, Marx claimed, it is unavoidable that the proletariat, or the working class, will revolt against the bourgeoisie.[2]

The bourgeoisie is made up of those who own and operate the factories and shops. Marx felt that the owners oppressed, or took advantage of, the working class.

During the Cold War, communism became a national obsession. Many Americans saw communism as an octopus-like creature that would take over the world if given the chance.

According to Marx, the proletariat was responsible for creating the products and wealth that the bourgeoisie enjoyed.[3]

Americans feared that communism would spread to the United States. Communism threatened the very way of life that Americans treasured. However, there were many Americans who felt that capitalism was unfair to the working class. One such man would become a central figure in America's case against Alger Hiss.

The Accuser—Whittaker Chambers

Whittaker Chambers was hardly the sort of person you might think would be at the center of a drama that involved the entire nation and divided American opinion. The Chambers family moved to Lynbrook, New York, a small rural town, in 1904. Whittaker was born near Prospect Park in Brooklyn, New York. His family did little to help Chambers fit in anywhere. In fact, Chambers was not born with the name that later became famous. His mother chose his birth name—Jay Vivian Chambers. Later, Chambers would choose to use his grandfather's name—Whittaker—instead of the embarrassing "Vivian." Chambers' father hated the name his mother gave him so much that he refused to say it aloud and called his son "Beadle," instead.[4] Throughout his life, Whittaker Chambers' father would become more and more distant from his family.

Chambers' family background made it additionally

difficult for Whittaker to be part of the rural town where he grew up. His father was an artist, and his mother had been an actress. Both professions were unusual in the simple town of Lynbrook and only served to set Whittaker farther apart from other children.

To make matters worse, Whittaker Chambers' mother, Laha, did not allow her overweight son to play with the neighborhood children. And, when the time finally came to send Whittaker, and his brother, Richard, to school, they were dressed in shirts with wide collars and ruffles and a large, floppy bow tie. Other children made fun of the unusual outfits.

Whittaker's father moved in and out of his family's life, caring for his growing sons grudgingly. Rather than purchase long pants for Whittaker when he entered high school, he gave his son his own used clothing. Perhaps it was in protest that Whittaker Chambers allowed his hair to grow to below his collar—something unheard of for young men in the 1920s. He often went several days at a time without bathing, which earned him the nickname "Stinky."

One thing his parents did provide for Chambers was a love of literature and languages. His early introduction to the French language paved the way for Whittaker to excel in languages. An attic full of his grandfather's collection of fine books provided the young Whittaker with a foundation for excellence in writing. Both skills proved very useful to Whittaker Chambers later in life, and, in fact, provided him with a means to earn a living.

Chambers Rebels

Besides refusing to wash, Whittaker Chambers also did not take care of his teeth, allowing them to become rotten and discolored. This neglect toward his personal appearance was a habit he continued throughout most of his adult life. Later, his poor teeth would result in his being identified in court.

However, these points of rebellion were not enough to satisfy Chambers. In his eighteenth year, Jay Vivian Chambers decided to leave home and make his own way in the world. He rejected his mother's plan of finding a "suitable" white-collar job, and bought a train ticket to Baltimore, which was as far as his money would take him. With ten dollars in his pocket, Chambers started a new life for himself. At the same time, he chose to use his grandfather's name—Whittaker.

Whittaker Chambers entered Columbia University in 1920, but his career there was troubled. His grades were good, but he often skipped classes. Then, in his third year of college, as editor of *The Morningside*, Columbia's literary magazine, Chambers wrote and published "A Play for Puppets."

A student delegation sent to complain to the president of the college called the play "filthy," and demanded that Chambers take back every single printed copy of the magazine and resign as editor.[5] Chambers refused, although he did leave college voluntarily.

In 1924, Whittaker Chambers returned to Columbia. However, as in the past, Chambers missed classes time after time, until he finally dropped out of college that same year.

Chambers' connection to Columbia came to a complete close in 1927. Although Whittaker Chambers had not attended classes there for some time, an investigator found fifty-six of Columbia's books that Chambers had stolen from the university's library. The school notified Whittaker Chambers that he was forbidden to ever return to the university.

Although Chambers did not finish his college career, he proved to be a bright student and gifted linguist, a person who learns many languages. Before leaving college, Whittaker Chambers published a number of poems and plays that showed his gloomy nature. His writings also demonstrated his growing attachment to the principles of communism.

When Chambers finally left school, it was to work for the Communist party publication, *The Daily Worker*.[6] He gradually worked his way up in importance at the newspaper, from a menial job as delivery boy to feature writer.

It was during his career at *The Daily Worker* that Whittaker Chambers married Esther Shemitz on April 15, 1931.[7] The couple had two children, Ellen and John. Esther Chambers would later become an important witness in the Hiss-Chambers case.

Eventually, the Communist party found Chambers valuable and trustworthy enough to remove him from his job at the newspaper. The party put him to work in the party underground. As a member of the underground, Chambers was no longer officially part of the Communist party. His work was done secretly. Chambers said that at first his job was to find other people for the Communist party and encourage them to become members.

Later, Chambers claimed that he did espionage work for the Communist party. As an espionage agent, he spied on his country. Chambers contacted employees of the U. S. government who were in favor of communism and asked them to provide any documents that came across their desks. Chambers would bring the papers to another location and photograph them himself during the night. According to Chambers, he would return the government documents to the U.S. employees the following day. Before anyone knew the papers were missing, they would be filed where they belonged.

Throughout this time, the Communist party supported Chambers. He did not have a "regular" job to pay his bills. Part of his responsibilities as an underground worker included staying out of the regular stream of life. He did not hold a paying job or pay taxes. Instead, the party paid him one hundred dollars each month and an additional sum of one hundred fifty dollars to cover the cost of a telephone, traveling, and living expenses. Whittaker Chambers was also cautioned never to go directly to a party-related meeting. He was to take a roundabout way to each encounter, to make sure that he was not being followed.

Chambers' Intellectual Break With the Party

Gradually, Chambers began to find disagreement with the Communist party. The party developed under the ideals of Marx and Lenin. Later, the Soviet Union found itself

Vladimir Lenin (left) and Joseph Stalin (right) were two of the men who helped to shape the Communist party.

governed by Joseph Stalin, a hard man with a stern manner and no pity for anyone he suspected of opposing his authority. Eventually, Whittaker Chambers came to understand that communism would not correct society's problems. Instead, Chambers saw that Communists were ruthless in their efforts to preserve communism.

Whittaker Chambers had heard of the "husbands torn forever from their wives in midnight arrests," of the execution cellars and torture chambers of the secret police.[8] He knew of trainloads of people, left on remote tracks to freeze to death in the Russian winter because they opposed the Communist state.

Although he had known of this suffering for some time, Chambers claimed that he was untouched by it until he listened with his "soul."[9]

Because of changes in both the Communist party and in himself, Chambers denounced communism and broke off communication with Communist party members. In 1938, he left behind the underground work that consumed his time and began to support himself by translating books from German to English for publishers. Soon, he found a job as an editor for the well-known magazine *Time*. Before long, Chambers had worked his way up to senior editor. He took advantage of this position to write many articles and essays attacking the Communist theory and system.

Although his position as senior editor of a significant magazine was an important job, Whittaker Chambers remained an inconspicuous man. He shuffled to and from work each day, sloppily dressed and still overweight. Few would have recognized the man by sight. Whittaker Chambers had written a great deal and was even a published author of plays and poetry, but none of his works received international attention. So, how did Whittaker Chambers suddenly become the center of attention throughout the world?

The answer is that Chambers was not completely without friends. In fact, he claimed to have had a friendship with someone who was unlikely to befriend such a person as Whittaker Chambers.

Alger Hiss—The Accused

If there could be anyone who was the opposite of Whittaker Chambers, it was Alger Hiss. Hiss graduated from Harvard Law School and went on to become an attorney. A smooth,

Oliver Wendell Holmes, Jr., was a Justice on the Supreme Court from 1902 to 1932. He was also a friend of Alger Hiss.

polished, and handsome man, Alger Hiss had many friends in important positions within the U.S. government. One such friend was Oliver Wendell Holmes, Jr., a Justice on the Supreme Court from 1902 to 1932.[10]

Alger Hiss served as Holmes' law clerk after law school. Clerkships are very important positions for a new graduate, and the competition for these jobs is very strong. As part of his responsibilities, Hiss would review particular cases that had been brought before the Supreme Court, and research the law that applies to that case. Hiss and other clerks would then submit their findings to a particular Justice. Based on that research and the Justices' knowledge of the law and the Constitution, the Justices would then rule on how the case should be decided.

Hiss continued to rise through the ranks in government jobs. From 1936 through World War II, he worked in various positions for the State Department. The State Department is the part of the American government that is responsible for relations with other countries and for foreign trade. As a member of the State Department, Hiss had access to many secret documents.[11]

Later in his career, Hiss helped create the United Nations. The United States, Great Britain, and the Soviet Union formed the United Nations in an effort to preserve whatever peace had been achieved after World War II. The international organization was meant to regulate relations among the world's countries, so that peace could be maintained. Alger Hiss was secretary-general of the 1944

Alger Hiss was a fairly high-ranking official in the American government. He is shown here (left) as President Harry Truman (right) shakes his hand at a United Nations Conference.

conferences that were held in San Francisco to form the United Nations.

In that position, he was responsible for more than one thousand delegates and their secretaries and interpreters. Hiss arranged for housing, communication, and transportation for this large group. He also saw to the needs of over one thousand members of the press who had come to report on this historic event. Alger Hiss continued to support the efforts of the United Nations. In 1946, Hiss left his position with the State Department to become president of the Carnegie Endowment for International Peace.[12]

The Carnegie Endowment was an organization that was made possible by the donations of Andrew Carnegie, a very wealthy American. Carnegie's intention was to hasten the end of international war, "the foulest blot upon our civilization."[13] Under Alger Hiss' direction, the Carnegie Endowment analyzed the way the United Nations worked, and prepared studies to help the United Nations with its organizational problems and any other challenges.[14]

These were the two main players in the drama that would captivate the entire country—Alger Hiss, the tall and handsome lawyer with a lifetime of public service to his credit, and Whittaker Chambers—the messy, inconspicuous man who publicly admitted to his past as a Communist party member.

The stories told by the two men were completely opposite. This one dispute caused two trials that captured the world's attention. In order to understand why the Alger Hiss case became so famous, it is necessary to know more about the relationship between America and the Soviet Union. The following chapter explains the uneasy way these two countries waged the Cold War.

chapter one

AMERICA FIGHTS THE COLD WAR

ESPIONAGE—Due to the friction and distrust that existed between the Soviet Union and the United States, both countries engaged in espionage, or spying on each other. The Soviet Union employed a number of agents to build a spy network. These spies would provide the Soviet Union with valuable information collected or developed by the United States.

Some of the agents were known as "legal" agents, or those who were Soviet citizens but living in the United States for a variety of reasons. A number of legal agents were journalists or people connected with the Soviet embassy. These agents would report information that could be collected by anyone with the time and inclination to do so.

One master Soviet spy, Rudolf Abel, collected most of the information he sent to Moscow from *The New York Times* and *Scientific American*. In fact, almost 90 percent of the information collected by spies can be found in public places.[1]

Nations also use "illegal" spies to engage in espionage. Illegal spies were Soviet men and women who were not in the United States on official business. These agents entered the country with forged documents and lived in America under false names. Often, the behavior and training of the "illegals" seemed very much like an old spy movie. During the 1930s, all Soviet illegal agents entering New York City stayed at the Hotel Taft in Manhattan. The "chief" of the illegal agents would greet the newcomers with a prearranged password: "Greetings from Fanny." If the response was, "Thank you. How is she?" the new agent was identified, and the training began.[2]

Congress Investigates Communist Activities in America

Americans were divided in their attitude toward reports of Communist activity in the United States. Many Americans felt that the "threat" of communism was not a risk at all.[3] It was simply a rumor that Communists were employed in high-level government positions.

Part of the disagreement stemmed from the various ways communism was defined. Opinions ranged from those who felt that Communists were simply those who wished to bring about changes in society, to those who thought of Communists as Soviet spies.[4] For those who defined Communists as Soviet spies, the threat was very real. To those people, Communist espionage in the United States was only the beginning of a political tidal wave that would sweep away the freedom enjoyed by Americans.

In response to these fears, Congress formed a committee

to investigate the rumors of Soviet espionage in America. The group was called the House Un-American Activities Committee (HUAC). Formed in 1938, the committee was also called the Dies Committee, named after the chairman, Martin Dies, of Texas. The HUAC was charged with the responsibility of investigating people and organizations that were suspected of presenting a danger to American security.

The Dies Committee quickly gained a bad reputation. The HUAC used questionable methods to root out Communists who held federal jobs, such as postal workers. A federal employee would be fired for treason or spying with little evidence. Such workers could also be let go for

Whittaker Chambers (standing far left in dark tie) appeared before the House Un-American Activities Committee. It was there that he repeated the charges that Alger Hiss had been a member of the Communist party. Hiss is standing sideways on the right.

belonging to an organization listed as being "subversive" by the Department of Justice. Subversive activities are designed to weaken or overthrow an existing government.

Proof that a person had committed these crimes against the country, or belonged to a "subversive" group, did not have to be very convincing. "Reasonable grounds for believing" these charges was enough.[5] The accuser did not have to be identified—the FBI wanted to protect the identities of their informants for other cases. The list of organizations labeled "subversive" by the attorney general could not be challenged, either by an accused individual or by the organization.

Charges of disloyalty to America grew quickly and reached all levels of society. The most noted of these trials were those involving Hollywood movie stars and writers. In 1947, ten Hollywood writers were subpoenaed, or commanded to appear, before the HUAC to answer charges of spreading Communist propaganda.

The ten defendants refused to answer the question "Are you now or have you ever been a member of the Communist Party of the United States?" Instead, all responded that they had the right to remain silent. They refused to say anything that might give the committee evidence that could be used against them. The defendants became famous as the "Hollywood Ten."

During the trial of the Hollywood Ten, E. B. White, author of *Charlotte's Web*, commented on the case. He complained the "men have been convicted, not of wrong-doing, but of wrong-thinking; That is news in this country and if I

WARNING
from the
FBI

The war against spies and saboteurs demands the aid of every American.

When you see evidence of sabotage, notify the Federal Bureau of Investigation at once.

When you suspect the presence of enemy agents, tell it to the FBI.

Beware of those who spread enemy propaganda!   Don't repeat vicious rumors or vicious whispers.

Tell it to the FBI!

J. Edgar Hoover, *Director*
Federal Bureau of Investigation

The nearest Federal Bureau of Investigation office is listed on page one of your telephone directory.

This warning from the FBI urged all Americans to report anyone they thought might be a Communist spy.

have not misread my history, it is bad news."[6] Those who defend the activities of the HUAC are quick to point out that congressional investigations are not held to the same standards as a court of law.

The "Show Trials"

While Americans watched the drama of the HUAC investigations unfold, members of the Communist underground and Soviet citizens faced their own troubles.

Stalin demonstrated his merciless rule to the world in the new laws he passed. Soviet children over the age of twelve faced the same punishment as adults for any crime. People who lived in Russia during this time would have been sent to a labor camp for eight years for stealing corn or potatoes, or five years for stealing cucumbers.[7]

However, Stalin's capacity for cruelty is best demonstrated by the "Moscow Show Trials." These trials were also known as the Purge. Stalin eliminated all challenge to his authority by bringing his political enemies to trial. These trials were charades,

In this poster from the Cold War era, the government was alerting Americans that even "innocent" gossip about national affairs could have serious results.

without any attempts to discover the truth. Hundreds of Communist party members and officers in the Soviet military were executed, sent to prison for long sentences, or banished to slave labor camps in Siberia.[8]

The Purge lasted from 1935 through 1938, leaving several hundred thousand men and women dead. Fear spread throughout the Communist party. Those who approached their superiors about the "rumors" of the bloody purge were quickly silenced. One American agent was warned, "A comrade who has just come back from Moscow is going around saying that there is a terror going on there and then they are arresting and shooting everybody. He should be taken care of."[9]

Soviet agents working in the United States were called back to the Soviet Union to answer flimsy charges of disloyalty to the Communist party. Slowly, those who had supported the "Great Revolution" in Russia began to believe that communism itself was not the answer to the world's problems. The social structure that American Communists trusted to save the world was now a threat to their personal safety.

Orders continued to come from Moscow headquarters, requiring agents to travel to the Soviet Union. More and more, American citizens working underground for the Communist party refused to obey those orders. One such American was Whittaker Chambers. Now a family man, Chambers questioned the purity of the Communist party and its activities.

Chambers decided that the Purge was just as wrong as

other great wrongs committed throughout history. He admitted to himself that "this is evil, absolute evil. Of this evil I am a part."[10] Having decided that, Chambers began to plot his break with the Communist underground, a long process he knew would be filled with danger.

The break was not an easy one. Whittaker Chambers had friends in the Communist party, a family to protect, and no immediate way to feed and shelter his wife and children. As an underground agent, he did not have a work history to present to a possible employer.

Also, there was the threat that he would be hunted down and executed by Soviet agents, for the security and secrecy of their network. Chambers was well aware that other dissatisfied Communists had been hunted down and executed for denouncing Stalin.[11] In order to survive his break with the Communists, Whittaker Chambers needed a plan.

Whittaker Chambers' Plan

Because Chambers had spent so long in the underground, few people outside the Communist party knew or cared about him. The lonely man had little contact outside his spy group. Hardly anyone would notice if Chambers suddenly disappeared. Therefore, Chambers knew that his only chance of safety was to make himself as visible as possible. He decided to rejoin society.

Chambers searched for a job and found employment with *Time* magazine. At the same time, he tended a farm in Maryland, commuting by train between city and countryside on a weekly basis. The job gave him the life in public that he needed for safety. The farm in Maryland gave him the physical exercise and contact with nature that he needed for relaxation.

Whittaker's Choice

Chambers had to do more than simply return to a life "above ground" to escape Stalin's executioners. Chambers felt he had an obligation to undo whatever strides he had helped the Communist party make in the United States. To accomplish that, Chambers needed to warn the American government of Communist party activity in America. The country had to know of Communist agents working in high-level government jobs and providing the Soviet Union with government documents.

On the other hand, warning the government exposed Chambers to a great risk. He would be admitting to spying on his own country. Would Chambers escape execution by the Soviets only to be charged as a spy and traitor to his own country? It was a difficult position, apparently one without a happy ending either way for Whittaker Chambers.

Whittaker Chambers Warns the American Government

Finally, the course of history led Whittaker Chambers to make his confession to the U.S. government. Although Joseph Stalin had been one of the world leaders who spoke out against Adolf Hitler, the Soviet Union and Nazi Germany signed a nonaggression pact on August 23, 1939.[12] This agreement provided that neither country would

Nazi Germany led by Adolf Hitler (marching in front of his troops) was free to invade Poland without any interference from the Soviet Union, following the signing of a nonaggression pact in 1939.

associate itself with any other country or group of countries that directly or indirectly threatened the other country.

Nazi Germany was now free to invade Poland without any interference from the Soviet Union. At the same time, the Soviet Union would be able to attack Finland, Lithuania, Latvia, and Estonia without any problems from Germany. With the European continent divided up this way, World War II was ready to explode.

Chambers was finally convinced of his duty to alert American authorities to the Communist underground and its activities in the American government. Now that the Soviets and Germans were allies, the Nazis would have the benefit of all the information that Chambers had sent to the Soviets. For Chambers, this was unthinkable.

Therefore, Chambers arranged a meeting with President Franklin Delano Roosevelt's assistant secretary of state, Adolf Berle, Jr. As assistant secretary of state, Berle was responsible for keeping President Roosevelt informed about intelligence matters.

Two days before, World War II had finally begun with Germany's breaking through the borders of Poland. Although the U.S. Army had not yet become involved in the fighting, Berle expected America to be part of the fighting within forty-eight hours and wanted government agencies to be "clean," or free of Communist infiltration.[13]

Whittaker Chambers shocked Berle by outlining the entire Communist underground ring operating in Washington, D.C. He also named several people and claimed that they were part of the Communist network.

Among those named were State Department workers Alger Hiss, Donald Hiss (Alger Hiss' brother), and Laurence Duggan. Berle knew each of these men personally.

Chambers and Berle left the meeting with very different feelings. Adolf Berle knew, like others, that many on Chambers' list were Communists. But membership in the Communist party was not a crime. Berle did not take the threat of communism seriously, thinking that these individuals were simply interested in Communist theories. He also felt that Chambers might not have been very accurate about the details.

Whittaker Chambers left the meeting with great respect for Berle and President Roosevelt. However, he feared that the government would take the easier course and punish *him* for his confessed espionage work. Chambers claimed that he

Whittaker Chambers (right) outlined the entire Communist underground spying operation in Washington. D.C.

never asked for immunity, or a promise from the govern-ment not to prosecute him, in exchange for his testimony.[14] In order to protect himself, Whittaker Chambers withheld some information from the committee. He tucked it away in Brooklyn, New York, and feared for the day he would have to use it.

America was certain to join the war at some point. Washington employees at every level were scrambling in an attempt to prepare for involvement in the world war. As a result, Berle did not follow through on Chambers' claims. Had Whittaker Chambers exposed himself to the risk of arrest, only to have his warning fall by the wayside? What Chambers did not know then was that he would have to wait until long after World War II had come to a close, before anyone paid attention to his warning.

For nearly ten years after meeting with Berle, Chambers lived in peace, working as a senior editor for *Time* magazine. However, the fact that he had committed treason, a crime against his country, continued to haunt him. For Chambers, treason was a "sin against the spirit."[15] That sin created a black circle of loneliness that could not be forgiven.[16] Chambers could not begin to repent for his "sin" until the HUAC decided to take his confession seriously. That would not happen until another ex-Communist, Elizabeth Bentley, made her own confession.

"I Shall Testify"

The ten years of peace for Whittaker Chambers came to an end on August 1, 1948. Through an old acquaintance,

Chambers learned that he had been subpoenaed, or called to testify, by the HUAC. At home with his wife that evening, Chambers told her that he might be called to testify. When Esther Chambers asked her husband what he would do, his response was simply, "I shall testify."[17]

A woman named Elizabeth Bentley had captured the attention of the press when she approached members of the HUAC with claims that many high-ranking Washington officials had been involved with the Communist party just prior to and during World War II.

Bentley was nicknamed "the Red Spy Queen" by the press, but she had nothing but her own sworn word as proof of her charges. The HUAC had gained the reputation of

Whittaker Chambers is shown here as he appeared before the House Un-American Activities Committee.

being an alarmist committee, sacrificing fairness and truth for dramatic effect. Then-President Truman believed that the hearings were a "red herring," or a way to distract Americans from the fact that Congress was not tending to its proper business of passing laws.

Therefore, members of the HUAC were reluctant to make another all-out effort to root out communism without corroborating, or supporting, testimony. Still, the public was interested in Bentley's testimony, so HUAC staff members searched for evidence to support her story. A review of FBI files turned up notes of an interview with Whittaker Chambers. Chambers was called to testify on August 3, 1948.[18]

Chambers' Testimony Reaches Public Ears

Once on the witness stand, Whittaker Chambers asked to read a statement, during which he described his history in the Communist party and his later work in the underground. He explained his reasons for breaking off from the underground and Communist philosophy. Chambers also told of the difficult times following that break, and that he had "lived in hiding, sleeping by day and watching through the night with gun and revolver within easy reach."[19]

Then, Whittaker Chambers named those he claimed had been part of the Communist party during Franklin Delano Roosevelt's presidency. Among those named were Nathan Witt, John Abt, Lee Pressman, and Alger Hiss. Chambers was careful to explain that the Soviets did not expect these people to commit espionage. The Communist party guessed that they would rise in American government and would be more valuable to the Communist cause than as members of a large secret group.[20]

The witness then recounted his efforts to encourage other members of the Communist party to break off their relationship with the group. Chambers claimed to have had a longtime friendship with Hiss. For that reason, Whittaker Chambers said he paid a personal visit to Hiss' home. During that visit, Chambers said he tried to get Alger Hiss to break with the Communist Party. According to Chambers, Hiss cried when the two friends separated, but his answer was final.[21]

The Confrontation

Reporters were astounded by what they had heard.[22] If Chambers' testimony were true, it meant that Communists had been in key positions throughout World War II and continued to hold positions of trust in government leadership. It meant that some of America's most respected people were bent on destroying America's form of government. Most of all, it meant that the HUAC's charges of Communist infiltration of the government were true.

The very day that Whittaker Chambers mentioned Alger Hiss' name before the HUAC, a reporter called Hiss at the Carnegie Endowment in New York, looking for Hiss' reaction. Alger Hiss took the charges seriously. He immediately sent a telegram to J. Parnell Thomas, HUAC chairman, about the statements made by "one Whittaker Chambers:"

I DO NOT KNOW MR. CHAMBERS AND, SO FAR AS I
AM AWARE, HAVE NEVER LAID EYES ON HIM.
THERE IS NO BASIS FOR THE STATEMENTS ABOUT
ME MADE TO YOUR COMMITTEE . . . I WOULD . . .
APPRECIATE THE OPPORTUNITY OF APPEARING
BEFORE YOUR COMMITTEE TO MAKE THESE
STATEMENTS FORMALLY AND UNDER OATH . . . ON
AUGUST 5.[23]

Contradiction

On August 5, 1948, Alger Hiss took the stand. He made a
stark contrast to his accuser. Hiss was sharp, well dressed,
and handsome. More important, Alger Hiss was perfectly
calm and relaxed, as if he were perfectly confident that the
charges of his involvement in spying would soon be swept
away.

Hiss began by reading a prepared statement. In that
statement, Alger Hiss denied having been a member of the
Communist party, and denied further that he agreed with any
of its teachings. He repeated his claim that he did not know
Whittaker Chambers: "To the best of my knowledge, I never
heard of Whittaker Chambers. . . . So far as I know, I have
never laid eyes on him, and I should like to have the opportunity to do so."[24]

Next, Alger Hiss commented on his impressive career,
from Harvard Law School through his years in government
service. Hiss appeared to feel that he should be above questioning, since he told the committee, "I think my record in
the Government service speaks for itself."[25]

Robert Stripling, the HUAC's chief investigator, showed

a current photo of Whittaker Chambers to Alger Hiss. Stripling said that Chambers was much heavier in the photo than he would have been in the days Whittaker Chambers claimed to have known Hiss. Alger Hiss replied that he had seen Chambers' pictures in the newspaper, and that the accuser "looked like a lot of people." In fact, Hiss stated, he might even mistake the man in the photograph for Karl Mundt, who was the acting chairman of the committee.[26]

The Reaction

When Alger Hiss stepped down from the witness chair, he received the congratulations of reporters and those who had simply come to watch the proceedings. Clearly, Hiss had performed with great confidence. In addition to his

Alger Hiss is shown here examining a photo of Whittaker Chambers. Hiss testified that he never knew a man by the name of "Whittaker Chambers." He claimed the man in the photo looked like a lot of people.

impressive work record, Hiss' calmness under questioning left little doubt in the minds of many that he had been wrongly accused.

However, not everyone was pleased with Alger Hiss' testimony. Already under criticism for their dramatic tactics and sweeping charges against questionable witnesses, HUAC members feared public condemnation. Even Robert Stripling commented on the very sharp contradiction in the testimony.

Some committee members, including Richard M. Nixon, a congressman from California, were not as impressed with Alger Hiss' testimony as was the press. Nixon complained that Hiss' attitude was "coldly courteous, and, at times, almost condescending." According to the young congressman, Hiss was "insolent," with a tone that was "insulting in the extreme."[27]

Before the committee pursued Alger Hiss, or any of the other alleged Communists, the HUAC decided to make certain that both Whittaker Chambers and Alger Hiss had a chance to double-check their identification of each other. HUAC members agreed that the best method would be a face-to-face meeting of the two men, in private.

Richard Nixon volunteered to make the arrangements and conduct the meeting.

Nixon's decision to take that responsibility would thrust the young congressman into the public spotlight and accelerate his political career. That fame would follow Nixon throughout his career, all the way to the White House, where he later served as president of the United States.

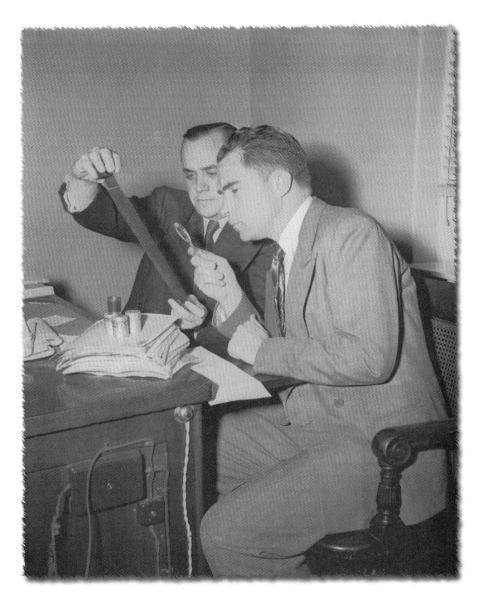

Richard Nixon (right) and an investigator for the House Un-American Activities Committee inspect the microfilm from the Pumpkin Papers. Nixon went on to become president of the United States.

Chambers Provides More Details

It seemed clear that either Whittaker Chambers or Alger Hiss was lying, since their stories were so sharply opposite. However, there was still a possibility that the disagreement could be explained by a case of mistaken identity. Therefore, Nixon attempted to clear up any possible mistakes by seeking details of Chambers' claimed friendship with Hiss.

With that in mind, Richard Nixon and the other members of the subcommittee met with Whittaker Chambers at the Federal Courthouse in New York City on Saturday, August 7, 1948. If Chambers could recall information that only a close friend would know, it might show that Hiss was lying. On the other hand, if Chambers failed to show enough knowledge of Hiss' personal life, it could show that Chambers was lying.

At that meeting, Chambers provided a great deal of information to the committee. Whittaker Chambers first told the committee that Alger Hiss did not know him by the name of "Whittaker Chambers," but by the name he used in the Communist underground—"Carl." Chambers also denied that Hiss was simply part of a group studying the theory of communism. According to Chambers, Hiss was committed to infiltrating the government in the interest of the Communist party. Furthermore, Chambers stated that he collected membership dues from Hiss and his wife, Priscilla, on a monthly basis.

The committee questioned Chambers about the Hisses' private life. Chambers told the subcommittee members of Alger and Priscilla Hiss' hobbies. They enjoyed bird watching and the theater. Whittaker Chambers always saw Alger Hiss' admission of sighting an extremely rare bird, a prothonotary warbler, as a key turning point in the case. He told of a black car with hand-operated windshield wipers that the Hisses had loaned to him from time to time. Whittaker Chambers also remembered Alger Hiss' purchase of a new car in 1936. At that time, Hiss turned his old car over to the party, so that it would be of use to some "poor organizer."[28]

Whittaker Chambers also gave specific details of different houses that the Hisses lived in. He provided information about their location, colors of the rooms, the furniture, and some of the vacations the Hiss family had taken. Chambers even claimed to have stayed overnight with the Hisses, as their guest. Later, Alistair Cooke, a newspaper writer, would comment that Chambers recollection of the Hisses' life could only have been made by the closest of friends, or by a "tireless detective job."[29]

By the time Richard Nixon had finished questioning Whittaker Chambers, the members of the subcommittee were convinced that the witness was telling the truth. However, it still remained necessary to question Alger Hiss further, to find whether there was any possible explanation for the differences in their stories.

Hiss Is Recalled

On August 16, 1948, Alger Hiss was recalled by the subcommittee for a final opportunity to resolve the differences between his and Chambers' testimony. Hiss denied knowing the man who claimed to be "Carl," or that he ever paid Communist party dues. Once again, Hiss was shown photographs of Chambers. He stated that it did not remind him of anyone he knew, but that the face was "not completely unfamiliar."[30]

During the questioning, Alger Hiss added that he was concerned about information being leaked back to Whittaker Chambers. Hiss feared that his testimony would be given to Chambers, who could then pretend to have known certain details all along. This would make Chambers appear more believable.

Robert Stripling told Hiss that the committee still had an open mind about his testimony so far, and pointed out that Chambers had "rattled off details" about Hiss' life for hours. At that point, Hiss suddenly stated that he had known a man named George Crosley, who had lived in his home for a period of time. Hiss described the man, mentioning that he had bad teeth. He also told the committee that Crosley may have no connection to the entire "nightmare."[31]

Committee member Edward Hébert noted that, up until Hiss heard of Whittaker Chambers' detailed testimony, Alger Hiss had been very cooperative. Hébert stated that Hiss had suddenly become defensive, concluding, "whichever one of you is lying is the greatest actor that America has ever produced."[32]

The Meeting

On August 17, 1948, Alger Hiss got the opportunity he and Richard Nixon requested. Whittaker Chambers and Alger

Hiss stood face to face in a room at the Hotel Commodore in New York City. Hiss identified Chambers as the man he had known as George Crosley, although Crosley's (Chambers') teeth had improved from the last time he had seen him. For his part, Whittaker Chambers denied ever having used the name of "George Crosley." However, Chambers did say that Alger Hiss was the man who was a member of the Communist party, and who had been his friend.

A witness for a congressional committee cannot be sued for his or her statements made to the committee. Therefore, Alger Hiss could not sue Whittaker Chambers for anything Chambers said to the committee. However, Hiss could sue Chambers for defamation if he ever repeated his accusations outside of the committee's presence. A person sues another for defamation when the defendant makes false statements about the other's reputation.

Hiss became angry and told Chambers to repeat his accusations outside of testimony. At that point, Hiss could freely sue Chambers and attempt to prove his innocence in court. Soon after, Whittaker Chambers appeared on the national radio talk show *Meet the Press*. There, Chambers repeated his accusations. Hiss replied one month later on September 27, 1948, by suing Chambers for $75,000.[33]

Defamation Suit Proves Costly

On November 4, 1948, Hiss' attorney, William Marbury, began questioning Whittaker Chambers. This is a formal procedure, where careful notes are taken in preparation for trial. In addition to questioning a witness, an attorney can also demand that the witness bring any documents or papers connected to the case. On November 4, Marbury asked Whittaker Chambers if he had any papers from any member of the Hiss family.

Chambers replied that he did not have the papers on him, but that he had not checked all possible places where he might have hidden them. After the second day of questioning, Chambers' attorney warned him "if [he] did have anything of Hiss' [he] had better get it."[34]

Chambers went to the Brooklyn house of Nathan Levine, his nephew. When Chambers broke with the Communist party, he had given a large bulky envelope to his nephew, who hid it in a dumbwaiter. A dumbwaiter is a very small elevator operated by a pulley system. Dumbwaiters were used in large homes to carry meals from the kitchen on one floor to the dining room on a different floor of the house. The envelope contained four slips of paper with handwritten notes, sixty-five typewritten pages, and five strips of microfilm.

When Whittaker Chambers returned to the hearing for further questioning, he gave the papers, both typewritten and handwritten, to William Marbury. However, Chambers did not give the rolls of microfilm to the attorney. The handwritten pages appeared to be in Alger Hiss' handwriting. The typewritten pages were copies of State Department reports.

Chambers claimed Hiss gave the documents to him in 1937. According to Chambers, Hiss took original State

Department reports home, where his wife would type copies. Alger Hiss would return the originals to his office the next day. Chambers sent the copies to Moscow.

The Pumpkin Papers

Alger Hiss immediately told his attorney to send the documents to the Department of Justice. They, in turn, notified the HUAC. The HUAC sent a telegram to Richard Nixon, who was on a Caribbean cruise on the steamer *Panama*. The telegram read:

> SECOND BOMBSHELL OBTAINED BY SUBPOENA 1 A.M. FRIDAY. CASE CLINCHED. INFORMATION AMAZING. HEAT IS ON FROM THE PRESS AND OTHER PLACES. IMMEDIATE ACTION APPEARS NECESSARY. CAN YOU POSSIBLY GET BACK?[35]

Nixon immediately called in a seaplane to bring him back to Washington. The American press greeted him in a rush, flashbulbs popping, to capture the image of the man who had been questioning Alger Hiss.

By the time Nixon arrived in Washington, Whittaker Chambers had already led Robert Stripling to his farm in Maryland. There, Chambers made his way to the pumpkin patch and opened a hollowed-out pumpkin. Inside were the five rolls of microfilm that Chambers had taken from the Brooklyn house of his nephew. Three of the rolls were undeveloped. Two, stored in waterproof bags, had been developed. The pumpkin contained pictures of documents, not actual paper documents. Still, the press labeled them the Pumpkin Papers.

Whittaker Chambers hid evidence that Alger Hiss had been a spy in a hollowed-out pumpkin on a farm in Maryland.

Alger Hiss' lawsuit against Whittaker Chambers had proven costly for Hiss. The handsome young man had filed the suit in order to prove his innocence. However, Hiss' tactic backfired, since it led to the appearance of the Pumpkin Papers. The federal government now considered Chambers' charges seriously.

However, Alger Hiss' alleged espionage had taken place so long ago, that Hiss could no longer be tried for espionage. A statute of limitations makes certain that criminal charges will be brought against a defendant when evidence is still likely to be available. If too long a period of time passes, a person charged with a crime may not be able to defend himself fairly. Documents are destroyed, and witnesses die or move away, making a defense nearly impossible.

This did not mean that Alger Hiss would go entirely unpunished if guilty. Hiss had stated under oath that he had not given State Department documents to Whittaker Chambers. He also testified that he had not seen the man he knew as George Crosley after January 1937. If Hiss were lying when he made those statements under oath, he would be guilty of the crime of perjury. However, it had to be proved that Alger Hiss had lied under oath. A New York federal grand jury was asked to evaluate whether Alger Hiss should be tried for perjury.

The grand jury found that there was enough evidence to require a trial. This does not mean that Hiss was found guilty of perjury. Rather, the United States of America was now permitted to bring Alger Hiss before a court of law for a trial to determine whether he was indeed guilty of the crime of perjury.

On May 31, 1949, Alger Hiss appeared in the United States District Court for the Southern District of New York, in Manhattan's Foley Square.[36] At this trial, he would answer the charges that he had lied under oath about engaging in espionage and having known Whittaker Chambers after January 1937. Judge Samuel H. Kaufman, a federal court judge, would preside over the trial. A jury would decide whether Hiss was guilty or innocent of perjury.

Thomas F. Murphy, an assistant United States attorney, prosecuted the case against Alger Hiss. As prosecutor, Murphy was responsible for proving the charges against Hiss. Murphy would analyze the evidence, question the

When Alger Hiss appeared before the grand jury, the jury decided that Hiss should be tried for perjury (lying under oath).

witnesses, and present the facts to the jury. It was Murphy's job to prove to the jury beyond a reasonable doubt that Alger Hiss had perjured himself. In order to do so, Thomas Murphy would have to show that Hiss did indeed commit espionage, and that he had known Whittaker Chambers.

Lloyd Paul Stryker represented Alger Hiss. A defense attorney does not have to prove that his or her client is innocent. In America, a criminal defendant is innocent until proven guilty. However, a good defense attorney cannot simply hope that the prosecutor will fail to prove the defendant's guilt beyond a reasonable doubt. Instead, the attorney will also question, or cross-examine, the witnesses for the government. By doing so, the defense attorney might create reasonable doubt in the mind of the jury, and the defendant can go free.

Stryker began his defense with a motion, or request to the judge, that the case against Alger Hiss be dismissed. Hiss' attorney told the court that the defendant's testimony came on the last day of the grand jury's "life." According to Stryker, this made Hiss' testimony somewhat unimportant. Lloyd Stryker argued that the matters on which Hiss had testified were not material to the grand jury's investigation, meaning that Hiss' testimony had little to do with the decision that the grand jury had to make.

Judge Kaufman considered the defense's motion and denied the request to dismiss the charges. Alger Hiss would have to stand trial before a jury of his peers, or equals.

chapter two

THE PROSECUTION'S CASE

COURTROOM—The trial was underway and the prosecutor along with the defendant's attorneys would be starting with their opening arguments. During this stage, each side tells the jury what it intends to prove during the course of the trial. Thomas Murphy spoke first. He faced the jury of two women and ten men. Murphy's initial comments to the jury went straight to the heart of the Alger Hiss trial—whether or not Whittaker Chambers, the chief witness against Alger Hiss, was to be believed.

The prosecutor told the jury that he wanted them to "examine Chambers. I want you to listen attentively; watch his conduct on the stand . . . because if you don't believe Chambers then we have no case under the federal perjury rule. . . ."[1] Next, Murphy invited the jury to "examine what motive he [Chambers] would have for lying, and I daresay you will be convinced as I am that he is telling the truth and that what Mr. Hiss told the grand jury were lies."[2]

Once again, Whittaker Chambers took the stand to tell under oath of his involvement with the Communist party. He described his methods for gathering State Department documents for delivery to the Soviet government. Once again, the witness testified that Hiss took State Department documents from the office and brought them home to his wife, who retyped them.

Chambers gave further details about his claimed relationship with Alger Hiss. Once, he explained, he was ordered to make certain gifts of money to those who worked closely with him. These gifts were supposedly from the Communist party, in gratitude for the work that the individual members of his espionage group, or "cell," had done. Whittaker Chambers said that he explained to his party authorities that men such as Alger Hiss did not engage in espionage expecting to be paid for their efforts, but out of a desire to serve the cause of communism.

Therefore, the witness explained, he purchased a number of beautiful and expensive Oriental rugs for gifts to his fellow Communist workers. Chambers explained that he delivered one of these rugs personally to Hiss.

Chambers also explained that Alger Hiss had loaned him his car and apartment. When he was in need of a new car, Chambers explained, the Hisses loaned him the four hundred dollars needed to purchase the vehicle. A bank president would later introduce evidence to show that Priscilla Hiss withdrew four hundred dollars from the

Hisses' account on November 19, 1937—about the same time Chambers claimed to have received the loan from Hiss.

Finally, Whittaker Chambers told of his attempt to convince Alger Hiss to break away from the Communist party. He explained that Hiss refused because of principle to stop working for the Soviet spy network.

Chambers Cross-Examined

The time had come for the defense to cross-examine Whittaker Chambers. During cross-examination, the attorneys for the other side in a trial ask questions of the witness concerning his or her testimony. The purpose is to show flaws in the witness's story, and to show that the witness is either lying or unreliable in some other way.

Lloyd Paul Stryker first confronted Chambers about his honesty. Stryker pointed out that Chambers had used many different names throughout his life, such as Jay Vivian Chambers, "Carl," and "Bob." Stryker suggested that the fact that Whittaker Chambers used so many different names showed that he was basically a dishonest person.

Attorney Stryker also pointed out that Chambers had been untruthful before the HUAC, the grand jury, and before Hiss' lawyers. Not only had Chambers denied being involved in espionage, Stryker told the jury, but Chambers had also denied earlier that Hiss was involved in espionage. It was not until Alger Hiss brought his suit for defamation that Chambers made such accusations against Alger Hiss. Stryker counted sixteen such lies. Chambers admitted to all of them.

Stryker also suggested that Whittaker Chambers had concealed evidence from the grand jury. The defense attorney noted that Chambers never delivered the Pumpkin Papers to the grand jury, but only revealed them when Hiss sued him for defamation. Trying to show that it was Chambers, not Hiss, who was the liar, Stryker asked "[t]hen you admit that you testified falsely, and committed perjury before the grand jury in this building, is that right?" Whittaker Chambers answered "[T]hat is right."[3]

This was an important admission from Whittaker Chambers. Chambers had admitted to lying, making his believability on the stand doubtful. If Chambers was an admitted liar, then how could the jury be expected to believe his testimony on the stand?

Many years later, Alger Hiss himself would point out the importance of this admission. "[H]e, the sole essential witness in a perjury case . . . publicly asserted at the trial that he had committed a series of perjuries before the very grand jury that had been induced to [charge] me because my testimony was in conflict with his."[4]

During cross-examination, Stryker tried to introduce two additional means of discrediting Whittaker Chambers. First, the defense attorney brought up Chambers' unhappy family history, noting that Laha Chambers, Whittaker's mother, had emotional problems throughout her life. He also brought out that his brother had committed suicide. The suggestion was that Whittaker Chambers, too, had emotional problems.

Throughout Chambers' testimony, Stryker had asked Dr. Carl Binger, a psychiatrist, to observe the witness's

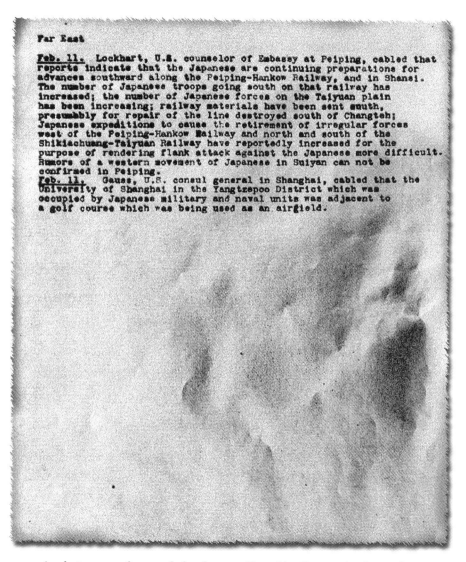

Far East

Feb. 11. Lockhart, U.S. counselor of Embassy at Peiping, cabled that reports indicate that the Japanese are continuing preparations for advances southward along the Peiping-Hankow Railway, and in Shansi. The number of Japanese troops going south on that railway has increased; the number of Japanese forces on the Taiyuan plain has been increasing; railway materials have been sent south, presumably for repair of the line destroyed south of Changteh; Japanese expeditions to cause the retirement of irregular forces west of the Peiping-Hankow Railway and north and south of the Shikiachuang-Taiyuan Railway have reportedly increased for the purpose of rendering flank attack against the Japanese more difficult. Rumors of a western movement of Japanese in Suiyan can not be confirmed in Peiping.

Feb. 11. Gauss, U.S. consul general in Shanghai, cabled that the University of Shanghai in the Yangtzepoo District which was occupied by Japanese military and naval units was adjacent to a golf course which was being used as an airfield.

A photocopy of one of the famous Pumpkin Papers is shown here. Whittaker Chambers hid these documents in a hollowed-out pumpkin on his farm in Maryland.

testimony. Binger complied with the request and watched Whittaker Chambers as he testified, taking thorough notes during the proceedings.

Lloyd Paul Stryker also pointed out Whittaker Chambers' two different versions of his delivery of the Pumpkin Papers to the FBI. When Chambers first delivered the microfilm to the FBI, he told them he could not recall how he got them. However, the defense attorney pointed out, he swore during Hiss' trial that he had received the rolls of microfilm from Alger Hiss. Which story was true? Stryker left the jurors to wonder whether Chambers was only now trying to identify Hiss as the source of the microfilm.

Redirect Examination by Murphy

After Lloyd Paul Stryker finished cross-examining Whittaker Chambers, it was the prosecution's chance for redirect examination. During redirect, an attorney can ask further questions that might explain any doubts created about the witness by the defense. Redirect also gives an opportunity for the witness to repeat his or her statements, so the jury can measure the truthfulness of the witness.

First, Mr. Murphy asked Whittaker Chambers to explain his reasons for withholding the Pumpkin Papers from the grand jury. The witness explained that he was simply trying to protect an old friend from prosecution by the U.S. government. Whittaker Chambers testified that he only wanted to destroy the progress of communism in America while doing no more damage than was necessary to the individual people involved.[5]

The Cold War led many Americans to fear an invasion by the Soviets. Here, school children practice their "duck and cover" drill. Children were led to believe that covering their heads and scrambling under their desks would protect them during a nuclear attack.

The prosecution ended its redirect by bringing out that Chambers himself had never been treated for mental illness. Whittaker Chambers left the stand, having finally reached his goal—alerting the American public to his perceived threat of Communist infiltration of the United States. The jury would have to hear much more testimony before it was allowed to discuss whether or not Chambers was telling the truth.

However, Americans not on the jury were free to judge Whittaker Chambers' testimony. Chambers clearly had convinced Nixon, Stripling, and Murphy that his claims about Alger Hiss and espionage were true. There were many others who were not convinced, their doubts aroused by the witness's unfortunate history.

Eleanor Roosevelt, the well-loved past First Lady of America, expressed this position best. As a friend of Alger Hiss, Mrs. Roosevelt pointed out the many "facts" about Whittaker Chambers as a witness. "One cannot help being mystified as to why [he] should be believed at all . . . he seems to have no hesitancy about telling various unsavory facts about his private life, which make him seem less and less valuable as a witness."[6]

Other Witnesses for the Prosecution

Whittaker Chambers was not the only witness that prosecutor Thomas Murphy brought to the stand. Several other witnesses testified about portions of Whittaker Chambers' testimony, either to confirm what he had said or to supply additional information about statements Chambers made on the stand.

One such witness was an executive from the bank Mr. and Mrs. Hiss used during the time Hiss supposedly was Whittaker Chambers' friend. The bank president testified that four hundred dollars was withdrawn from the Hisses' account on November 19, 1937. This was during the same time Chambers claimed Hiss gave him a loan in order to buy a new car.

A car salesman took the stand to state that Mrs. Chambers appeared at his dealership on November 23, 1937. On that date, Esther Chambers traded in an old car and made a cash payment of $487.65 in exchange for a new car. The trade was made only four days after Priscilla Hiss withdrew the four hundred dollars from her joint account with Alger Hiss.

Nathan Levine, Esther Chambers' nephew, also took the stand. He stated that, indeed, Whittaker Chambers had come to his home in Brooklyn, New York, to retrieve a packet left in his dumbwaiter years earlier. Levine recalled that he had hidden the package at Chambers' request.

Esther Chambers was next to take the stand as a witness for the prosecution. She was a nervous woman with thick glasses, who dressed plainly and wore no makeup. Esther Chambers' farm-toughened hands proved her many years of hard work tending the Maryland farm. She spoke quietly on the stand, but she had a vivid memory.

Chambers told of her friendship with the Hisses, recalling in detail the many occasions on which the two families had visited. She also described the Hiss apartments specifically, including the furnishings and wall color. She even recalled the floral pattern of the bedspread in the master bedroom of the Hisses' last home, before her husband broke away from the Communist party.

Lloyd Stryker cross-examined her about her opinion that her husband was a "great and decent man." Stryker questioned whether it was decent to plot to overthrow the government of his own country for twelve years. Esther Chambers rose to her husband's defense. "I believe that he is a great man, who lives up to his beliefs. His beliefs may change, as they did!"[7]

More Evidence

Finally, the jury and spectators were going to see the evidence that had caused such a commotion. All four handwritten notes and sixty-five typewritten pages of the Pumpkin Papers were read into evidence.

Prosecutor Thomas Murphy called Walter H. Anderson to the stand. Anderson was the chief of the State Department's Department of Records. As chief of this department, Walter Anderson was responsible for keeping files of State Department records and documents. In his hand, Anderson held the original reports, cables, and memos that had apparently been used by whoever made the type-written copies.

Walter Anderson summarized the nature of the notes and typewritten sheets. The documents were incoming telegrams from American embassies overseas and notes made of diplomatic conversations. The "spy papers" also included reports of Japanese troop movements during World War II. Anderson explained to the jury that although some of the documents were "non-sensitive," or not secret, others were classified as "Code D." These were the most sensitive of the State Department's documents.

Anderson said that even though many documents might not be of any value to the Soviets as they were, they had a more subtle use to America's enemy in the Cold War. Historians of Hiss' day noted that research is like a crossword puzzle. And, since "no outsider can say what particular piece of information may supply the other side with the key to its problem . . . any leakages have to be jealously guarded against."[8]

The witness also showed that Alger Hiss could have been the person responsible for stealing the Pumpkin Papers, since they had passed through Hiss' office at some time. Anderson showed the jury the initials "AH" in the margin of two of the documents. Many others went through Assistant Secretary of State Francis Sayre's office. Hiss was Sayre's assistant during the time the spy papers traveled through Sayre's office.

This evidence seemed to point directly at Alger Hiss. But once again, a witness for the prosecution was cross-examined by the defense. This time, Lloyd Stryker's partner, Edward McLean, handled the questioning. On cross-examination, Anderson admitted that as many as thirty-five copies might be made of any document that came through the State Department. Even more helpful to Alger Hiss,

Anderson admitted that security in the State Department offices was not very tight. Perhaps ten people could have had access to the unlocked file cabinets.

The FBI Testifies

Lloyd Paul Stryker had already admitted that the handwritten Pumpkin Papers were in Alger Hiss' handwriting. However, the prosecution still had to connect Alger Hiss to the typewritten documents. Thomas Murphy called FBI agent Ramos C. Feehan to the stand to make this connection.

Making the connection was a very difficult task. The FBI could identify the typewriter used to make the copies as a Woodstock model. Each typewriter has its own peculiarities. If the typewriter used to produce the Pumpkin Papers could be found, the FBI could establish a connection between Hiss and the spy papers. However, FBI agents had searched for the missing typewriter and could not locate it. There was still one other way to make that connection, and Feehan told the jury how he had done so.

On the stand, Feehan compared the typewritten Pumpkin Papers to samples of typing that Priscilla Hiss had produced for a private school. Ramos Feehan showed the jury ten of the letters. The letters showed that several of the typewriter's letters fell below the line of type and a particular key struck the page at an uneven amount of pressure from one side of the letter to the other. For all but one of the documents, Feehan testified that the same typewriter that produced the

Pumpkin Papers also produced the letters that were prepared by Mrs. Hiss.

The defense team had no questions for Ramos. The prosecution rested, or stated that it had concluded its presentation of the case to the jury. The evidence against Alger Hiss had taken shape over the course of several witnesses' testimonies. The last witness had supplied very strong evidence that seemed to connect Alger Hiss to the spy papers.

However, the defense team had yet to make its own presentation of the facts. Would Lloyd Stryker and his cocounsel be able to show other facts proving Hiss' innocence? The jury had to wait only through the weekend to hear the beginning of the Alger Hiss story.

chapter three

THE CASE FOR THE DEFENSE

WITNESSES—Before Lloyd Paul Stryker called any witnesses to the stand, he revealed a startling piece of information to the jury. The FBI had several agents looking for the typewriter that was used to produce the Pumpkin Papers—so far with no success. However, Stryker declared to the jury, "We have the typewriter in our possession."[1]

Stryker suggested that a "guilty man" would not have informed the FBI about the location of the typewriter and offered it for examination, if it would damage his case.[2]

If the many press members, and crowd of curious public were looking forward to seeing Alger Hiss testify at the start of his case, they were disappointed. Beginning on June 20, 1949, Mr. McLean, Lloyd Paul Stryker's cocounsel, began the defendant's case.[3] Rather than the well-known Hiss, an impressive chain of well-known and respected people came to the stand to testify about Alger Hiss' good reputation for truthfulness and loyalty to his country. Among those who testified were:

- John W. Davis, a former presidential candidate and trustee of the Carnegie Endowment;

- Dr. Stanley Hornbeck, Hiss' chief at the State Department during World War II;

- Charles Fahy, former solicitor general of the United States;

- Judge Charles Wyzanski, a district court judge from Massachusetts;

- Justice Felix Frankfurter, Associate Justice of the Supreme Court of the United States; and

- Justice Stanley Reed, Associate Justice of the United States Supreme Court.

The next witness to take the stand was Claudie Catlett, a woman who had worked for the Hiss family as a maid. Catlett testified that she remembered a man who called himself "George Crosby" once visiting the Hiss family. Claudie Catlett also recalled many useful items the Hisses gave her over the years, usually as the Hiss family prepared to move to a new address. One of the articles was a typewriter that the Hisses gave her children when they moved to Thirtieth Street on July 1, 1936.

This testimony was important. If Alger Hiss had indeed given the typewriter to Claudie Catlett in the middle of 1936, then Priscilla Hiss could not have produced the

Pumpkin Papers on that machine during the time Whittaker Chambers claimed.

When Murphy cross-examined Catlett, however, she admitted that she did not "remember no typewriter at all."[4] Later, the witness stated that she remembered the machine only after the FBI interviewed her, and that one of her sons told her the Hisses made a gift to them of the typewriter.

When Catlett's son, Perry, followed her to the stand, he recalled that the Hisses gave him the typewriter when they moved to their house on Volta Place in November 1936. Perry Catlett also remembered carrying the machine to a repair shop on K Street, because it was in poor condition.

The defense suffered another blow when Murphy rose to cross-examine Perry Catlett. The prosecutor told Catlett that the Woodstock repair shop on K Street did not open until September 1938. Murphy asked the witness if that would cause him to remember bringing the machine there after that date. Perry Catlett replied only that he did not know—he remembered only that he had taken it there for repair.

This admission was an important development in the case against Alger Hiss. If Hiss still had the Woodstock typewriter as late as 1938, then Priscilla Hiss could still have produced the Pumpkin Papers on that machine, as Chambers claimed. In the face of this admission, Alger Hiss would finally take the stand.

Alger Hiss Takes the Stand

Although a defendant does not have to take the stand to testify in a criminal trial, Alger Hiss chose to do so. On

Thursday, June 23, 1949, Hiss had the opportunity to answer the charges against him publicly. Lloyd Stryker led Alger Hiss through a narration of his career, accenting the many achievements, connections to powerful people, and his part in the many historic milestones during his years as a public servant.

The defendant finally addressed the charges against him. He denied that he was ever a member of the Communist party; he denied giving any documents to Whittaker Chambers; he denied lying under oath; and he denied that he had ever asked his wife, Priscilla, to type any of the documents that would come to be known as the Pumpkin Papers.

Although the defense team admitted that the handwritten notes from the Pumpkin Papers were in Alger Hiss' handwriting, Hiss explained the reason for having made them. One of Hiss' duties in the State Department was to keep Mr. Sayre informed of all the material that came to his office. According to Alger Hiss, he would weed out the most important information to bring to Sayre's attention. In order to accomplish this task, Hiss stated, he made handwritten notes of the memos and reports. Hiss suggested that a thief may have given the papers to Chambers, since security was very relaxed.

When Stryker asked Alger Hiss about his friendship with Whittaker Chambers, the defendant said that he knew his accuser only as "George Crosley." He admitted befriending Crosley, who introduced himself as a writer and later leased his apartment and an old car. Hiss testified that "Crosley" failed to pay the rent, and that he last saw the man in August

1936. Hiss never saw the man who later gave his name as Whittaker Chambers until they met again in the Hotel Commodore in 1948.

Finally, Lloyd Stryker completed the questioning of his client by giving Alger Hiss another chance to deny the charges against him. "[I]n truth and in fact you are not guilty?"[5] Alger Hiss answered slowly, emphasizing each word. "I am not guilty."[6]

Murphy Cross-Examines Hiss

The prosecution's cross-examination of Alger Hiss was a painstaking confrontation between two men trained for courtroom procedures. Hiss threw off Murphy's concentration with interruptions that ranged from correcting Thomas Murphy's grammar, to pretending to misunderstand Murphy's fairly obvious questions.

Thomas Murphy did, however, draw two points from Alger Hiss during this troublesome exchange. First, Hiss admitted having received an Oriental rug in 1936 from Chambers, whom he knew as George Crosley. This admission was important, because Chambers testified that he had given such a rug to Hiss as a gift from the Soviets. Second, Alger Hiss denied knowing Hede Massing, a woman who was an admitted member of the Communist underground. This denial would not become important until much later in Alger Hiss' troubling history in court.

Finally, Alger Hiss stepped down from the witness stand. He remained calm and confident throughout the entire ordeal, strengthening the belief of many that he had been wrongfully accused. The next witness to take the stand was Alger Hiss' wife, Priscilla Hiss.

Priscilla Hiss Testifies

One of the important issues in the Hiss trial was that Whittaker Chambers claimed to have had a friendship with Alger and Priscilla Hiss. Hiss claimed only to have known Chambers as "George Crosley," and only for a brief period of time. Whittaker and Esther Chambers attempted to prove their relationship with the Hiss family by giving detailed descriptions of the various homes of the Hisses.

When Priscilla Hiss took the stand, she tried to make the jurors doubt that Mr. and Mrs. Chambers knew anything of the Hisses' private life. Priscilla began by contradicting Esther Chambers' description of her homes. Although Mrs. Chambers claimed confidently that the living room had been pink, Priscilla Hiss testified that both the walls and woodwork were green.

Esther Chambers had also testified that there was paneling in the dining room, but Priscilla Hiss stated firmly that there was no paneling in the dining room. Priscilla Hiss also testified that the Chamberses had never visited the Hisses' home on Volta Place, and that she had never visited any of the Crosley homes at all.

At Lloyd Stryker's questioning, Priscilla Hiss told the jury that she never made typewritten copies of any State Department documents at her husband's request. She also denied delivering any typewritten or handwritten notes to the man she knew as George Crosley. Although Priscilla

Alger Hiss is shown here later in his life. He died at the age of ninety-two, still proclaiming his innocence.

Hiss admitted owning the typewriter that produced the spy papers, she claimed she and her husband disposed of the machine in the fall of 1937. This would have been before the time the Pumpkin Papers were produced.

Four Hundred Dollars

It fell to Priscilla Hiss to explain the four-hundred-dollar withdrawal from her account. Whittaker and Esther Chambers both claimed that the Hisses loaned them that same amount in November of 1937. The loan of such a sum of money would indicate a friendship between the Hisses and the Chambers.

Unless Priscilla Hiss could convince the jury of a more innocent reason for the four-hundred-dollar withdrawal, the defense of her husband would suffer a serious blow. Priscilla Hiss testified that, at the time of the withdrawal, she was planning the move from her Thirtieth Street home to the house on Volta Street. The Volta Street house, she explained, was roomier and would need more furniture.[7]

Priscilla Hiss counted off a list of furnishings from her memory. In addition to curtains, rugs, lamps and a new dress, the housewife mentioned several new pieces of furniture that were needed. Stryker asked whether these purchases took up the entire four hundred dollars. The witness replied: "I am afraid it did."[8]

Finally, Stryker asked Priscilla Hiss whether she had ever lost her purse while she lived at Volta Place. Hiss answered that she had lost her purse, with her house key inside. With that, Stryker gave the jury something to wonder about—had someone used the key to enter the Hisses' household to type the spy papers?

Murphy Cross-Examines Priscilla Hiss

Thomas Murphy began his questioning of Priscilla Hiss by going over her use of the four hundred dollars. Hiss testified that she had several charge accounts in Washington, D.C., but that she paid cash for all the items she needed for the move to Volta Place. By the time she had moved into the new home, the entire four hundred dollars was gone.

Although Priscilla Hiss denied that she was a member of the Socialist party, Murphy showed her a copy of the registry of voters for 1932. After her name, the registry showed the notation "Soc." Hiss answered that she thought she was indicating whom she meant to vote for. During the 1932 election, she planned to vote for the Socialist candidate. At that point, Thomas Murphy asked the witness if she knew that the Morningside (an area of Manhattan) branch of the Socialist party had her listed as a member on their records. Hiss replied that she "certainly did not know that."[9]

Murphy also brought out inconsistencies in Priscilla Hiss' testimony. She said that she disposed of the Woodstock typewriter in December of 1937, before her move to Volta Place. However, when the FBI questioned her before the trial, she said that she could not recall how she had disposed of it.

Little by little, Thomas Murphy revealed that Priscilla Hiss was not being entirely truthful on the stand. When he asked about her typing skills, she responded that she was not very good, because she still "had to look at the keyboard to find a lot of the letters."[10] Murphy produced a transcript of her grades from her days at Columbia University. Priscilla had earned a B in her typing class.

Murphy raised Esther Chambers' testimony that Priscilla Hiss had taken a nursing course at the University of Maryland. The prosecutor produced a letter from the university about Priscilla's enrollment in that course. The letter was dated May 25, 1937. This was one year after the time that the Hisses claimed to have seen the Chambers family for the last time.

The unraveling of Priscilla Hiss' story took its toll. Although her husband remained cool and collected under questioning, Priscilla Hiss was shaken by Murphy's contradiction of her testimony. According to one courtroom observer, the witness's eyes were "dead as raisins in a circle of dough," by the time she left the stand.[11]

Priscilla Hiss was finally allowed to leave the stand, but her testimony had been different from her sworn statements to HUAC members on so many points. Had these inconsistencies harmed her husband's case? Mrs. Hiss would have to wait until the jury deliberated to find the answer to that question. In the meantime, Lloyd Stryker had other witnesses to call to the stand.

Dr. Carl Binger Is Called to the Stand

While Whittaker Chambers was on the stand, those in the courtroom noticed a man in the observers' section who was watching Chambers very carefully. The man had been taking notes throughout Chambers' testimony. Courtroom observers and reporters finally learned his name when Lloyd Stryker called Dr. Carl Binger to the stand, and this man rose.

Dr. Binger was a psychiatrist, called to testify as to Whittaker Chambers' mental stability as he appeared on the stand. Binger was also expected to give an opinion about possible motives Chambers might have for accusing Hiss of espionage. As psychiatric testimony was unusual in 1949, many lawyers did not trust these doctors as experts. Therefore, Murphy objected strongly when Dr. Binger took the stand.

Judge Kaufman decided that he would allow Binger to testify. However, he would allow the doctor to respond to questions from the defense only after the judge decided that Binger could answer them. Dr. Carl Binger took the stand and began by telling of his impressive medical training.

Lloyd Stryker asked whether Dr. Binger had observed Whittaker Chambers during questioning. Dr. Binger replied that he had. Lloyd Stryker then posed a hypothetical question. Hypothetical questions are asked of expert witnesses in a trial. These questions are a combination of assumed facts or circumstances. The set of facts mirror the questioning attorney's theory about a particular issue in the case. An attorney will compose such a question, asking the witness to assume a certain set of facts is true. Once the question has been presented to the expert, the attorney will ask for the witness's opinion.

Stryker's hypothetical question recalled the many

distasteful aspects of Whittaker Chambers' life. Stryker mentioned Chambers' unsanitary appearance during his childhood and Chambers' watching through the night with a gun at his side, waiting for the Communist party's assassins to attack. It took Lloyd Stryker forty-five minutes to state his question.

With the assumed "facts" presented, Stryker then asked Dr. Binger whether he had, after observing Chambers on the stand, formed an opinion as to Whittaker Chambers' mental condition. Before Dr. Binger could respond to the question, however, Murphy was on his feet to object. A jury is supposed to decide for itself whether or not a witness is believable. If Dr. Binger responded to Stryker's hypothetical question, Murphy feared, the jury might simply take Dr. Binger's judgment as their own.

The jury was not to hear Dr. Binger's answer. Judge Kaufman ruled that the information about the case is clear enough for the jury, "using its experience in life, to appraise the testimony of all of the witnesses who have appeared in this courtroom."[12] Dr. Carl Binger left the stand, but those who had been disappointed over Judge Kaufman's ruling would have another opportunity to hear Binger's expert opinion. With Dr. Binger's exit from the courtroom, Lloyd Stryker stood and told the judge that the defense rested.

Repairing Damage

Now that both the prosecutor and the defense had presented their witnesses, the time had come for rebuttal. Rebuttal witnesses are sworn in to repair any damage made to their case by the opposing side's witnesses. This evidence can explain or contradict testimony or evidence given by the opposite party.

The prosecution called one such witness. The witness's name was Hede Massing. Mrs. Massing was a known member of the Communist party. Mr. Murphy hoped to have Hede Massing testify that she knew Alger Hiss, and that he had been a member of the Communist underground.

However, Judge Kaufman ruled that Massing would not take the stand. He agreed with Lloyd Stryker that Massing's testimony had nothing to do with the question of when Hiss had last seen Chambers and whether he had given him stolen documents. Stryker also feared that Hede Massing's testimony would prejudice the jury against Alger Hiss.

This decision was a serious problem for the prosecution. Without Massing's testimony, there would be no one to support Whittaker Chambers' word that Alger Hiss had been a member of the Soviet spy network; and the jury already had good reason to doubt Chambers' word.

There was little else the attorneys could do to persuade the jury. All the evidence that the judge would allow had been presented and explained to the jury. Before Judge Kaufman sent the case to the jury for deliberation, or discussion, Stryker and Murphy each had one last chance to remind the jurors of their strongest arguments. This last chance is called the summation, or closing arguments.

chapter four

THE SUMMATION

WRAPPING UP—It was July 6, 1949, the twenty-fifth day of the Alger Hiss trial. Whatever arguments could be made on behalf of the defendant would have to be made now. Lloyd Stryker faced the jury and began his final effort to prove Alger Hiss innocent of perjury. That assault began with an attack on the character of Whittaker Chambers, Hiss' only real accuser.

According to Stryker, Chambers was a "recognized and accomplished perjurer, a liar by habit, by teaching, by training, by inclination and by preference."[1] Stryker was quick to point out the sordid past of the prosecution's main witness—dismissal from his library job for stealing books, his admitted espionage, and his time as a disbeliever in Christ.[2]

Hiss' defense attorney turned to the physical evidence against Hiss. The notes in the defendant's handwriting were only "trivia"; the microfilm, a "mess"; the Woodstock typewriter thrown out even before the spy documents were typed. As for the "friendship" between the Hisses and the Chamberses, Stryker called the idea "incredible."

Finally, Lloyd Stryker turned to his client and spoke to Alger Hiss directly. "[T]his long nightmare is drawing to a close. Rest well. Your case, your life, your liberty are in good hands."[3] Lloyd Stryker had completed his presentation of the case. He thanked the jury and returned to his seat.

The Prosecution Sums Up

For his closing argument, Thomas Murphy avoided the issues of emotion and the reputation of his witness, Whittaker Chambers. Instead, Murphy focused on the facts and the physical evidence. He also tried to overcome the obstacle of Hiss' fine reputation. Yes, Alger Hiss had a fine reputation and had called on many important Americans to swear to his honest character. But, Murphy pointed out, reputation was not everything. Benedict Arnold was once a respected officer, Lucifer was an angel that had once traveled within the sight of God. Murphy mentioned that Judas Iscariot was one of Jesus' chosen twelve, and he had betrayed Jesus. The prosecutor told the jury that Alger Hiss was a man very like the others who had wonderful reputations. "What," Murphy asked the jury, "was the name for such a person? . . . He is a traitor."[4]

More important to Murphy was the credibility of the four hundred dollars being used for shopping. At this point, Murphy faced the two female jurors and asked whether they would have paid cash for everything if they had charge and checking accounts. "Is that the way you do it . . .? Do you take the $400 out in one lump? . . . You might as well pay by check. Is that $400 explanation reasonable to you or is it just another lie?"[5]

Murphy's astonishment may seem overdone to you, but remember that the value of four hundred dollars in 1937 was very different from today's value. In terms of what that money would be worth today, Priscilla Hiss claimed to have withdrawn almost five thousand dollars at one time.

Next, the prosecutor listed the many facts that the defense could not answer. First, Priscilla Chambers knew too much about the Hisses not to have been closely involved with the family. She had described the Hiss household and knew of Priscilla's nursing course and the Oriental rug.

As for the Woodstock typewriter, Alger Hiss was caught in a lie as soon as the spy documents were produced. Rather than confessing his guilt, Hiss turned a near disaster to his own advantage. He produced the Woodstock typewriter at trial. An innocent man would certainly never deliver a piece of evidence that could prove his guilt. Since he was the first to "yell 'cop'" he must surely be innocent.[6] But, Murphy pointed out, this was only Hiss' way of preserving his image of innocence. The handwritten notes were not what Hiss claimed them to be, either. They were not summaries made to assist Francis Sayre, but complete copies of secret State Department papers.

The handwritten notes from the Pumpkin Papers had not been crumpled and thrown into a wastepaper basket, as Alger Hiss had claimed. Murphy held up one of the pages.

"That is a paper that was thrown into a wastepaper basket? With those creases?"[7] Neither was there any mystery as to the way in which the paper left Hiss' office, as the defense had suggested. Without speaking, Thomas Murphy folded the page along the creases before the jury. Still silent, Murphy tucked the tiny square of paper into the breast pocket of his suit jacket.[8]

Thomas Murphy finished his summation by admitting the many differences between Hiss and Chambers, and the differences between their wives. "Mrs. Chambers is plain and severe. Mrs. Hiss is demure and attractive, and intelligent . . . very intelligent." But these were emotional facts that had nothing to do with the many real facts that the jury had to consider. Murphy asked the jury to face their obligation to examine the issues side by side.

The trial was nearly at an end. After many months of preparation and waiting, Alger Hiss would soon discover whether he would be free or jailed as a convicted perjurer and believed Communist spy. He would have to wait only as long as it took for the jury to look at the facts and vote guilty or not guilty.

chapter five

THE CASE GOES TO THE JURY

DECISION—The attention in the courtroom now turned toward the panel of jurors. The twelve men and women heard seventy-three witnesses tell of the conflict between Alger Hiss and Whittaker Chambers. Hiss' fate now rested in the hands of a panel of jurors. Those jurors would be required to put their personal feelings to the side and decide the case based only on what they had heard in the courtroom.

Judge Kaufman turned to the two women and ten men selected for this task and began to explain the job before them. He gave the guidelines they should follow in order to reach their conclusion. This is called "charging the jury."

Judge Kaufman began his comments by reminding the jury that the Hiss case was famous, and that there had been a great deal of comment about it, in the newspapers, radio, and television. He realized that they would have to be "more than human" if they had managed to avoid any comment about it outside the courtroom.[1] However, they were to consider only the testimony and evidence that had been presented during the trial.

Next, Judge Kaufman told the jurors that they were to decide only whether Alger Hiss was guilty of the actual charges against him. Those charges were that Hiss had falsely testified before the grand jury on two matters. First, that he did not turn any confidential documents over to Whittaker Chambers or any other unauthorized person. Second, that he had not seen Whittaker Chambers after January of 1937, when he was said to have given the secret documents to Chambers.

If the jury found that Hiss did turn secret documents over to Chambers, then they should find him guilty of perjury on the first count. He would be guilty of the second count of perjury if the jury found that Hiss had delivered documents to Chambers in February and March 1938.

Beyond a Reasonable Doubt

Judge Kaufman told the jury that in order to find Hiss guilty of one or both of the counts against him, they would have to decide that the prosecution proved the case against Alger Hiss "beyond a reasonable doubt." This meant "a doubt based upon reason," but not "beyond a shadow of a doubt."

In addition, Judge Kaufman instructed the jury to consider a number of facts regarding Whittaker Chambers' testimony, since Chambers' truthfulness was crucial to the case.

- He had admitted lying, even under oath;

- he did not turn over the spy papers to the grand jury although he should have;

- he had been a Communist;

- his code of ethics and behavior on the witness stand;

- he had held a position of responsibility with *Time* magazine;

- and the believability and logic of his testimony.

Judge Kaufman then explained to the jury a point of law. Under the perjury law, no one could be convicted of perjury unless there were two separate witnesses testifying against the defendant, or one witness who was supported by other types of evidence, such as documents. If the jury found that they did not believe Whittaker Chambers, they were "instructed to find a verdict of not guilty in favor of the defendant."[2]

Alger Hiss' Character

Then, Judge Kaufman told the jury members that they must also consider certain points about the defendant's character.

- Hiss' life and education;

- his standing in the community;

- the conduct of the defendant before the grand jury;

- his explanation about the typewriter and documents.

Kaufman told the jury that other witnesses' testimonies about Alger Hiss' good character could allow the jurors to form a reasonable doubt as to the charges, when there might otherwise not be one. However, he reminded the jurors that "as each one of us knows, a man may commit a crime even though he was theretofore a person of good character."[3]

Finally, Judge Kaufman told the jury that the verdict must be a verdict of all twelve jurors. All jurors had to agree on whether Alger Hiss was guilty of one or both charges of perjury. They were to listen to each other and decide the matter to the best of their ability. Before the judge sent the jury members to deliberate, or discuss the case, he told them he was "confident that each of you will exert every effort to come to a just conclusion."[4]

At 4:20 P.M., on July 7, 1949, twelve people entered the juryroom to decide the fate of Alger Hiss.[5] The jury discussed the case for less than six hours, stopping for dinner and requesting several pieces of evidence. At 10:30, Judge Kaufman called the jury members back and asked if they felt they would reach a verdict in a reasonable amount of time, or if they preferred to go to a hotel for the night.

The jury's foreperson, Hubert James, reported that he saw no immediate verdict. Since people outside the case might have influenced the jurors if they were allowed to return to their homes, the twelve jurors were sent to a nearby hotel.

Messages From the Jury

On July 8, 1949, the jury returned to its task. Before long, however, Judge Kaufman received a note from Mr. James, which the judge read aloud. "The jury feels that it cannot reach a verdict." The judge told the twelve men and women that they had to try again. Therefore, in the late afternoon, the jurors returned once again to the job of determining Alger Hiss' fate.

Only one hour later, the jury sent another note to the judge, claiming that it could not reach a verdict. Alger Hiss, his attorneys, the prosecutor, and all others connected with the case had spent nearly a year preparing for the trial. Once

Senator Karl Mundt is shown here. He was a member of the House Un-American Activities Committee. Mundt displays the headline from a newspaper reporting that Alger Hiss was found guilty.

they reached the point that the case was given to the jury, they must have expected a decision in a short period of time. How could the jurors have been so far apart, that they felt they could not reach a decision?

Once again, the judge addressed the jury, explaining that he did not expect anyone to change his or her position simply to arrive at a verdict. However, if the jurors could not agree, it might mean that the case would have to be tried over again. This would mean a great expense for both the government and the defendant. They were asked to make yet another effort, and the jurors left the courtroom once again.

At 9:00 P.M. on the second day of deliberations, the jury reported for the final time that it "was impossible" to reach a verdict.[6] The judge reluctantly allowed the jurors to leave the courtroom, having thanked them for their service. Before they left the jury box however, he asked one of the jurors what the vote had been. "Eight to four, for conviction," he was told.[7]

Two months of trial had left the defense, prosecution, and the judge exhausted, and still, the matter was unresolved. Alger Hiss left the courtroom with a "keen dizzy look about his eyes," holding tight to Priscilla's arm.[8] For Alger Hiss, though, the long-awaited end to the trial was yet to come.

chapter six

THE SECOND TRIAL

BACK IN COURT—After many months of lengthy preparation, and an agonizing trial, Alger Hiss was required to endure a second trial. The Fifth Amendment to the United States Constitution promises Americans that they will not be tried more than once for the same offense. Since the jury in Alger Hiss' first trial had not reached a decision, the trial had not been completed. Therefore, the prosecution was free to conduct another trial, without placing Alger Hiss in the predicament of "double jeopardy."

After the end of Alger Hiss' first trial, his defense attorney, Lloyd Paul Stryker, told Hiss that he could probably get another "hung jury" but not an acquittal. That was not good enough for Alger Hiss, who later wrote that Stryker's "colorful" style did not agree with him.[1] It also seemed to Hiss that Stryker's constant "hammering at Whittaker Chambers' many perjuries and disloyalties . . . came at the expense . . . of sufficient attention to the details" of the spy papers.[2]

For the second trial, Alger Hiss chose Claude B. Cross, a law school classmate, to represent him. The defense team also included Edward McLean from the first trial. Judge Henry W. Goddard, an elderly man, "presided over his orderly court with complete authority and dignity."[3] Once again, Alger Hiss' trial took place in the United States District Court for the Southern District of New York. The proceedings began on Thursday, November 17, 1949.[4]

As you might expect, Alger Hiss' second trial was very much the same as his first trial. The important differences were that two controversial witnesses were allowed to take the stand. This time, Hede Massing was allowed to take the stand to testify for the prosecution. Judge Goddard made different decisions about witnesses' testimonies in the second trial.

Hede Massing, a self-confessed ex-Soviet agent, had not been allowed to testify during Hiss' first trial. Once on the stand, however, Hede Massing said that she, too, had known Alger Hiss to be an underground Communist. Massing testified that she and Alger Hiss had discussed whether she or Hiss would recruit a man named Noel Field into the ranks of the Communist underground.[5]

During cross-examination, Claude Cross managed to show that Massing had a poor memory for people, dates, and events. Cross also told the jury that Hede Massing had lied under oath during her husband's citizenship hearings.[6]

Case for the Defense

Like the prosecution, the defense team was also allowed to call a witness who had not been allowed to testify during the first trial. Judge Goddard allowed Dr. Carl Binger to take the stand. This time, Cross posed his own hypothetical question—which took the attorney sixty-five minutes to read to the witness.

The question essentially asked Binger whether his observation of Whittaker Chambers at both trials allowed him to form an opinion about Chambers' mental condition.[7] Binger replied that he thought, "Mr. Chambers is suffering from a condition known as psychopathic personality."[8] The most noticeable features of that disorder, Binger testified, were "repetitive lying and a tendency to make false accusations."[9]

Binger Cross-Examined

Whittaker Chambers' testimony was very important to the prosecution. The defense, however, had stripped away part of Chambers' believability as a witness. Could Thomas Murphy repair whatever damage Dr. Binger had caused on the stand? Murphy would have the opportunity to rebuild Chambers' reputation by cross-examining Dr. Carl Binger.

Of course, we cannot look into the minds of the jurors so many years ago, but it would be hard to imagine that Dr. Binger's harsh judgment of Whittaker Chambers' mental condition had no effect on the jury. Even so, Thomas Murphy's cross-examination was simple in its approach. Murphy did not try to argue with Binger about the validity of the science of psychiatry. Rather, the prosecutor's approach was limited to a common-sense approach. In later years, Murphy's questioning of this witness came to be recognized as an outstanding example of a cross-examination of a witness.[10]

During cross-examination, Murphy was able to draw several points from Binger:

- He could not form a complete opinion about a person's personality based upon his observation of that individual on the witness stand;[11]

- Binger could not know which of the assumptions in Cross' hypothetical question were true or untrue;[12]

- "Psychopathic personality" is a vague term; and[13]

- Other doctors could disagree with his opinion of Chambers' mental health.[14]

Dr. Binger also admitted that he had sometimes been wrong when making a diagnosis, or evaluation, of a patient's mental health.[15] Murphy had made his point with the jury, and Dr. Binger stepped down from the witness stand. Once again, the last witness had been heard.

It was nearly time for the court to turn the matter over to the jury members, with high hopes that they would this time reach a verdict. Before Judge Goddard charged the twelve jurors, however, Thomas Murphy addressed the issue of Alger Hiss' fine reputation. He told them: "I ask you ladies and gentlemen what kind of a reputation does a good spy have? Of course it must be good. The fox barks not when he goes to steal the lamb. It has to be good. But we are here on a search for truth. We are not concerned with reputations. . . ."[16]

Judge Goddard turned to the twelve jurors and told them they could consider the testimony of the psychiatrist, but that they were not to replace their own judgment with his. Finally, Judge Goddard asked them to consider all the evidence carefully and bring back a verdict.

Second Jury Deliberates

On January 20, the jurors retired to the jury room to discuss Alger Hiss' case. Only two hours later, the jury returned, not with a verdict, but with a request. The jurors asked to see the Pumpkin Papers and wanted to hear the court reporter reread the testimony of Mrs. Hiss, the Catletts, and all the testimony about the move to Volta Place. The judge patiently explained that this would require the court reporter to read testimony for five days.

The jury changed their request, asking only for the spy papers, the testimony of the Catletts about the time they received the typewriter, and Mrs. Hiss' testimony about the time she gave the typewriter away. The jury left again, this time with the requested evidence.

The following day, the jurors went back to work, only to return to the courtroom at 2:48 P.M. Courtroom reporters and observers expected further requests for evidence.[17] However, the solemn look on the jurors' faces could mean only that the ordeal was over. They had reached a verdict.

The Verdict

Judge Goddard asked the foreperson if the jury had reached a verdict. She answered simply that they had. The judge began to ask what they had decided, but the nervous foreperson cut in quickly and said "[g]uilty on the first count and guilty on the second."

After the many months of tension, courtroom drama, and public debate, there was nothing but astonished silence, and one gasp of surprise.[18] Alger and Priscilla Hiss sat quietly, although both were pale.[19] Judge Goddard thanked the jury for its time and told the jurors he thought that they had come to a "just verdict."[20]

The Sentencing

On January 25, 1950, Alger Hiss returned to the federal courtroom in New York City and stood before Judge Goddard.[21] The day had come for his sentencing, or the public announcement of the punishment that the judge would impose. Before Judge Goddard told Hiss about his sentence, however, the defendant's attorney asked Judge Goddard to grant Alger Hiss a new trial. Cross claimed that the judge made errors in the way he charged the jury. Judge Goddard denied Cross's request.

The next business in the courtroom had Cross and Murphy debating once again. Cross asked the court not to impose a prison sentence on Alger Hiss. Cross explained that the defendant had already suffered public shame, and that he was ruined financially. Alger Hiss spent all of his savings during the first trial and was able to pay for the second trial only with the support of his many friends.[22]

Cross added that there would always be lingering doubt as to Hiss' innocence "until the true and complete facts" came out.[23] Murphy answered at once that the defense had had two chances to bring out the true and complete facts. It was not quite fair now, he argued, to "add . . . some air of mystery." Judge Goddard settled the debate by telling Cross that Alger Hiss had received a very fair trial. The judge ordered Alger Hiss to rise and allowed the defendant a chance to speak before his sentence was imposed.

Alger Hiss faced the judge and made his prepared statement: "I would like to thank your Honor for this opportunity again to deny the charges that have been made against me. I want only to add that I am confident that in the future the full facts of how Whittaker Chambers was able to carry out forgery by typewriter will be disclosed."[24]

The American public had been following the progress of Hiss' courtroom drama since Whittaker Chambers first made his charge against the defendant in August 1948. With Hiss' statement to the court, there was little hope that the jury's verdict would close the *United States* v. *Alger Hiss* case. Many Americans still believed that Alger Hiss was innocent in spite of what the jury had decided. His mysterious comment about Chambers' "forgery by typewriter" would fan the flame of public interest in his case.

The federal law against perjury allowed Judge Goddard to sentence Alger Hiss to a maximum of five years. Hiss was found guilty on two counts of perjury, so he could possibly receive two sentences of five years each. Goddard imposed the maximum sentence, but he ordered that Hiss would serve the sentences concurrently, or at the same time. However, this does not mean that Alger Hiss was led directly to a jail cell to begin serving his sentence.

The judge released Alger Hiss on bail, until such time as he made an appeal to a higher court. Under this arrangement, a sum of money known as bail was deposited with the court. Hiss was allowed to be free until an appeals court decided whether he had received a fair trial. The bail was a kind of guarantee that Alger Hiss would make all necessary appearances in court and obey all laws while he was free. Otherwise, the money was lost. Still a free man, Alger Hiss continued his effort to clear his name.

The Appeal

Once a jury has found a person guilty, the case is closed. The convicted person may, however, ask another court, a court of appeals, to review the trial. The appellate court may decide whether there were any errors on matters of law, such as improper charges to the jury, or whether there was new evidence that could not have been obtained at the time of the trial. Only in very rare cases will the appeals court grant a motion for a new trial.

However, the appeals court can never substitute its own decisions about matters of fact for the decisions made by the jury. Findings of fact would include whether a witness was telling the truth on the stand. In Alger Hiss' case, a finding of fact would also include whether the Woodstock typewriter in evidence was the machine that produced the Pumpkin Papers.

Another law school classmate, Chester Lane, led Alger Hiss' appeal. Appeals are made by presenting a brief. This document contains all the reasons for the defendant's belief that a new trial should be granted. Chester Lane's brief argued that there were several reasons why Alger Hiss should be granted a new trial:

- Chambers' accusations were not adequately backed up by documents;

- Chambers' charges were proven lies, because the witness was an admitted perjurer;

- Hede Massing should not have been allowed to testify; and

- Thomas Murphy's inflammatory questioning of the witnesses prejudiced the jurors against Hiss.

A three-judge panel made its decision, which was written by Judge Harrie B. Chase and announced on December 7, 1950.[25] The opinion simply stated that Hede Massing's testimony was admissible. Chase's written opinion also judged that there was nothing in Thomas Murphy's conduct that would justify reversing the decision of the trial jury. Any doubts about Judge Goddard's charge to the jury were put to rest: "We find no error in it."[26]

The Next Step

Alger Hiss had one last option to have a court review his case. His attorney, Chester Lane, asked the Supreme Court of the United States to review the case. The Supreme Court is not required to review all cases that are presented to the highest court in America. It selects only those cases that involve a question regarding Constitutional law or an unsettled point of law in the federal courts.

On March 12, 1951, the Supreme Court denied Lane's request to review the case.[27] Of the nine Supreme Court Justices, only two voted to hear the case. Two justices, Frankfurter and Reed, did not vote at all, since they had been witnesses for Hiss during his first trial. The Supreme Court would not be reviewing Alger Hiss' case.

With all possible chances for appeal denied, Alger Hiss

With all possible chances for appeal denied, Alger Hiss had to enter prison. He is shown here on his way to prison.

had to enter prison. On March 22, 1951, Alger Hiss, once a high-ranking, respected government official, entered a federal prison in Lewisburg, Pennsylvania. He was required to have his "mug shot" taken and was identified as "inmate number 19137." [28] Hiss was also disbarred, or stripped of his license to practice law. Alger Hiss began serving his five-year sentence.

Asking for a New Trial

From behind prison walls, Alger Hiss continued to protest that he was innocent. He assisted his attorneys as they prepared yet another brief, asking Judge Goddard, who presided over his second trial, to grant yet another trial. The request, or motion, was filed on January 24, 1952.[29]

This request for a new trial was based on the claim that new evidence had been uncovered in the Hiss case. The new evidence followed through from Alger Hiss' mysterious statement before his sentencing, that Whittaker Chambers had committed "forgery by typewriter."

According to Hiss' latest defense team, scientific evidence showed that the Woodstock typewriter was a fraudulent piece of evidence. This was in spite of the fact that it was the defense team at Alger Hiss' first trial that tracked down the typewriter and presented it to the court with the statement that it had belonged to the Hiss family.

Chester Lane's brief claimed that

> the typewriter in evidence at the trials—is a fake machine. I . . . will be able to produce at the hearing, expert testimony that this machine is a deliberately fabricated job, a new type

face on an old body. This being so, It can only have been planted on the defense by or on behalf of Whittaker Chambers as part of his plot for the false [accusation] of Alger Hiss.[30]

The defense did not know Whittaker Chambers' reasons for committing "forgery by typewriter." As Chester Lane explained in his brief, he still did "not know exactly what Chambers did, or how he did it, or exactly what motivated him to frame Alger Hiss."[31] Lane guessed that Chambers might have been trying to protect himself in the defamation suit. However, the defense attorney was quick to point out, this effort may have involved "other people, and far larger objectives than the mere framing of Alger Hiss."[32] Lane did not specify what those objectives might be.

This latest motion for a new trial was also denied on July 22, 1952. Judge Goddard explained that the defense had shown no evidence to support their theory that Chambers had constructed the Woodstock typewriter used in evidence during Hiss' trials. Goddard swept away the theory, pointing to the far-fetched nature of Chambers' supposed plot.

Even if Chambers was able to construct "a duplicate machine, how would he have known where to plant it so that it would be found by Hiss?"[33] Judge Goddard's decision closed the last door of hope that Alger Hiss' name would be cleared in America's court system. However, this did not mean that the case of Alger Hiss passed quietly into history. Over the coming decades, many Americans would stubbornly insist that Hiss had not been a Communist spy.[34]

chapter seven

AFTER THE VERDICT

PRISON LIFE—Alger Hiss entered Lewisburg prison, knowing that it would probably be his home for the next five years of his life. When the last of his appeals failed, the probability that he would serve the full length of his sentence grew stronger. However, Hiss impressed prison officials with his work habits. His evaluations stated that he was dependable and "very outstanding."[1] Hiss also seemed "to be taking his incarceration in the form of an enforced vacation rather than a penitentiary sentence."[2]

Hiss' behavior earned him a valuable benefit. Those prisoners who follow prison rules can be released after serving about three fourths of their sentence for "good behavior." Alger Hiss left prison after forty-four months of his anticipated sixty-month sentence. However, for the remaining sixteen months, Hiss would be on conditional release. During the conditional period, Hiss would have to avoid "drunkenness, a brush

Alger Hiss (left, smiling) served forty-four months in prison before being released on November 27, 1954.

with the law, failure to report to [his] parole officer, [or] traveling without permission" beyond the allowed New York City area.[3]

Hiss Maintains His Innocence

Without his license to practice law, Alger Hiss had difficulty earning a living. He eventually found work as a stationery salesman and separated from his wife, Priscilla. Over the years, the man who was once in the spotlight of American news finished his attempts to clear his name by publishing two books about his life and trials. Alger Hiss died at the age of ninety-two on November 15, 1996. His accuser, Whittaker Chambers, had died thirty-five years earlier of a heart attack. Still, the Alger Hiss story arouses passionate debate between those who always believed he was innocent and those who believed he was guilty.

In 1992, Hiss supporters were uplifted with a new spark of hope. The Russian General Volkolgonov, who had been chief of the KGB archives, agreed to make a search of his files. He announced that he had come across no evidence to support the theory that Alger Hiss spied for the Soviet Union. Critics later complained that Volkolgonov examined only part of the documents in the archives. The Russian general admitted that he had not made an exhaustive search.

The Venona Project

Year after year brought additional forms of "proof" for supporters of each side of the Hiss-Chambers case. One such breakthrough was the release by the American

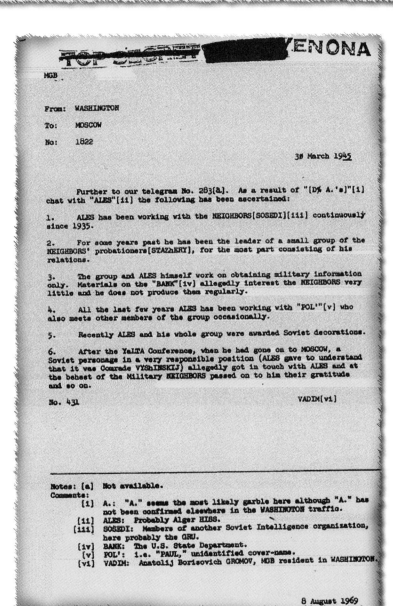

MGB

From: WASHINGTON

To: MOSCOW

No: 1822

30 March 1945

Further to our telegram No. 283[a]. As a result of "[D% A.'s]"[i] chat with "ALES"[ii] the following has been ascertained:

1.   ALES has been working with the NEIGHBORS[SOSEDI][iii] continuously since 1935.

2.   For some years past he has been the leader of a small group of the NEIGHBORS' probationers[STAZhERY], for the most part consisting of his relations.

3.   The group and ALES himself work on obtaining military information only. Materials on the "BANK"[iv] allegedly interest the NEIGHBORS very little and he does not produce them regularly.

4.   All the last few years ALES has been working with "POL'"[v] who also meets other members of the group occasionally.

5.   Recently ALES and his whole group were awarded Soviet decorations.

6.   After the YaLTA Conference, when he had gone on to MOSCOW, a Soviet personage in a very responsible position (ALES gave to understand that it was Comrade VYShINSKIJ) allegedly got in touch with ALES and at the behest of the Military NEIGHBORS passed on to him their gratitude and so on.

No. 431   VADIM[vi]

Notes: [a]   Not available.
Comments:
    [i]   A.: "A." seems the most likely garble here although "A." has not been confirmed elsewhere in the WASHINGTON traffic.
    [ii]   ALES: Probably Alger HISS.
    [iii] SOSEDI: Members of another Soviet Intelligence organization, here probably the GRU.
    [iv]   BANK: The U.S. State Department.
    [v]   POL': i.e. "PAUL," unidentified cover-name.
    [vi]   VADIM: Anatolij Borisovich GROMOV, MGB resident in WASHINGTON.

8 August 1969

This copy of a cable from Washington to Moscow from the Venona files is dated March 30, 1945. Venona analysts noted that "ALES" was probably Alger Hiss.

government of thousands of documents contained in the Venona Project. The Venona Project was a project of the National Security Agency (NSA) during World War II.

Code Names and Top Secret Documents

Venona workers intercepted and tried to decipher secret Soviet messages. In 1995 and 1996, the NSA declassified almost three thousand Soviet messages, or cables. This meant that documents that had once been classified as "top secret" were now available to anyone who wished to examine the cables.

One such document dated March 30, 1945, refers to an agent code-named "ALES." Soviets in Washington sent the cable to Moscow to inform the government there that "ALES" had "been working with" the underground "continuously since 1935." Further, the cable stated that "ALES" worked specifically on obtaining military information.[4]

Most compelling was the note that after leaving the Yalta conference, "a Soviet personage in a very responsible position" passed on to "ALES" their gratitude. At the bottom of the declassified document, Venona workers added their notation that "ALES" is "probably Alger Hiss."[5] Alger Hiss supporters would be quick to point out that Venona analysts merely stated that it was "probably" Hiss.[6]

However, the evidence continued to grow as the years went by. In 1996, two writers reported the results of their research for a book on Soviet spies. They uncovered notes from Soviet interviews of Noel Field, who had been questioned during Stalin's Moscow "Show Trials." Field told his

TOP SECI

Another individual who apparently was close to Wallace, and who is mentioned in the information from ▓▓▓▓▓▓▓▓▓▓ as an individual designated by the cover name of Frank. Frank was reported to be considering resigning from the State Department as of July 22, 1944, for "personal reasons." The identity of Frank has not been developed to date in view of the fact that the only available information is to the effect that he was well acquainted with Wallace and was to resign as of that date. However, it is interesting to note that Laurence Duggan (deceased), mentioned by Whittaker Chambers and Heda Massing, did resign from the State Department in the latter part of July, 1944. We have investigations in progress to identify both Jurist and Frank.

ALGER HISS (u)

According to ▓▓▓▓▓▓▓▓▓▓ on March 30, 1945, Anatoli B. Gromov, First Secretary and MGB representative at the Soviet Embassy in Washington, D. C., informed his Moscow headquarters that Ales had, for some years, been the leader of a little group working for Soviet Military Intelligence. It was stated that this group was composed mainly of Ales' relatives and that the group, which apparently was centered in the State Department, was working mainly on developing military information only and the information from the State Department interested them very little. It was stated that Ales, after the Yalta conference, had been in touch with a high Soviet official whom Ales implied was Comrade Vishinsky who thanked Ales on behalf of Soviet Military Intelligence. It would appear likely that this individual is Alger Hiss in view of the fact that he was in the State Department and the information from Chambers indicated that his wife, Priscilla, was active in Soviet espionage and he also had a brother, Donald, in the State Department. It also is to be noted that Hiss did attend the Yalta conference as a special adviser to President Roosevelt, and he would, of course, have conferred with high officials of other nations attending the conference. An attempt is being made by analysis of the available information to verify this identification.

THE COMMUNIST PARTY (u)

The ▓▓▓▓▓▓▓▓▓▓ information reflects that the Soviets were able to make extensive use of the Communist Party, USA, both for recruitment and for checking on various individuals regarding whom the MGB wanted information. Earl Browder was known by the MGB under the cover na▓

(u) CAUTION ▓ this must not be disseminated ▓ ▓ ▓ without approval of Mr. Ladd.

TOP SECRE

- 8 -

This copy of Venona analysts' report states reasons for deciding that "ALES" was probably Alger Hiss.

interrogators that Hiss did intelligence work for the Soviet Union. Noel Field added that Hiss had tried to recruit him, although he was already working for the Soviet underground.[7]

Clearly, Americans are still interested in Alger Hiss. The relationship between the United States and Russia brings out just as much controversy as the Hiss-Chambers case. Some Americans feel strongly that the Russians are our devoted allies, and that the tensions between our countries have relaxed a great deal. Still others claim that a completely friendly relation between the countries is merely wishful thinking.[8]

What do you think? Overall, the stories told by Whittaker Chambers and Alger Hiss remain sharply opposite to this day. Look over the evidence again and ask yourself what you would have believed, and what you would have decided.

Questions for Discussion

1. As you were reading about the evidence presented by both the defense and the prosecution, did you find any arguments more persuasive than the others? What made that particular piece of evidence so compelling?

2. Imagine that you were on the jury in the first Hiss trial. Would you have voted guilty or not guilty? Then, explore the facts of the case again. What would opposing counsel in the case have to show you in order to convince you to change your vote?

3. In recent years, the government of the United States released information that many historians believed finally proves Alger Hiss' guilt. Still, some people maintain that Hiss was innocent. What do you think accounts for this loyalty?

Chapter Notes

Introduction

1. Karl Marx, *The Communist Manifesto* (Appleton, Wis.: American Opinion Book Services, 1974), p. 36.

2. Ibid., p. 7.

3. Ibid., p. 9.

4. Sam Tanenhaus, *Whittaker Chambers* (New York: Random House, 1997), p. 3.

5. Ibid., p. 32.

6. Ibid., p. 49.

7. Ibid., p. 66.

8. Whittaker Chambers, *Witness* (Washington, D.C.: Regnery Publishing, Inc., 1952), p. 14.

9. Ibid., pp. 13–14.

10. Robert Famighetti, ed., *The World Almanac and Book of Facts* (Mahwah, N.J.: World Almanac Books, 1996), p. 92.

11. Alger Hiss, *Recollections of a Life* (New York: Arcade Publishing, 1988), p. 86.

12. Paul Moses, "Four Decades Later: Russian General Declares Man Accused by Nixon Was No Spy," *Newsday*, October 30, 1992, p. 5.

13. Alger Hiss, *In the Court of Public Opinion* (New York: Alfred A. Knopf, 1957), p. 3.

14. Ibid.

Chapter 1. America Fights the Cold War

1. Norman Polmar and Thomas B. Allen, *Spy Book: The Encyclopedia of Espionage* (New York: Random House, 1998), pp. x–xi.

2. Allen Weinstein and Alexander Vassiliev, *The Haunted Wood* (New York: Random House, 1999), p. 33.

3. William Manchester, *The Glory and the Dream* (Boston: Little, Brown and Company, 1974), p. 492.

4. Ibid., p. 489.

5. Ibid., p. 495.

6. Edward Knappman, ed., *Great American Trials* (Detroit: Mich.: Visible In Ink Press, 1994), p. 435.

7. James Trager, *The People's Chronology* (New York: Henry Holt and Company, 1992), p. 832.

8. Ibid., p. 845.

9. Whittaker Chambers, *Witness* (Washington, D.C.: Regnery Publishing, Inc., 1952), p. 76.

10. Ibid., p. 80.

11. Weinstein and Vassiliev, pp. 44–45.

12. Martin Walker, *The Cold War* (New York: Henry Holt and Company, 1995), p. 31.

13. Sam Tanenhaus, *Whittaker Chambers* (New York: Random House, 1997), p. 161.

14. Chambers, p. 457.

15. Ibid., p. 524.

16. Ibid.

17. Ibid., p. 530.

18. Paul Moses, "Four Decades Later: Russian General Declares Man Accused by Nixon Was No Spy," *Newsday*, October 30, 1992, p. 5.

19. Robert G. Whalen, "Hiss and Chambers: Strange Story of Two Men," *The New York Times*, December 12, 1948,

<http://www.english.upenn.edu/~afilreis/50s/hiss-chambers-nyt.html> (February 7, 2001).

20. Allen Weinstein, *Perjury* (New York: Random House, 1978), p. 5.

21. Chambers, pp. 72–73.

22. Alistair Cooke, *A Generation on Trial* (New York: Alfred A. Knopf, 1952), p. 57.

23. Weinstein, p. 8.

24. Alger Hiss, *In the Court of Public Opinion* (New York: Alfred A. Knopf, 1957), p. 9.

25. Weinstein, p. 10.

26. Tanenhaus, p. 226.

27. Weinstein, pp. 15–16.

28. Chambers, p. 377.

29. Cooke, p. 66.

30. Ibid., p. 67.

31. Ibid., p. 70.

32. Tanenhaus, p. 249.

33. Hiss, p. 157.

34. Ibid., p. 159.

35. Susan E. Evans, "The Alger Hiss Case: The Real Trial of the Century," October 31, 1995, <http://www-paradigm.asucla.ucla.edu/DB/Issues/95/10.31/view.hiss.html> (February 7, 2001).

36. Hiss, p. 199.

Chapter 2. The Prosecution's Case

1. Minutes of First Trial, *United States v. Alger Hiss*, "First Trial," (Wilmington, Del.: Scholarly Resources, Inc., June 1, 1949), p. 24.

2. Ibid., p. 25.

3. Ibid., p. 301.

4. Alger Hiss, *In the Court of Public Opinion* (New York: Alfred A. Knopf, 1957), p. 215.

5. Minutes of the First Trial, p. 529.

6. Eleanor Roosevelt, "Who is on Trial—Chambers or Hiss?" *New York World Telegram*, June 8, 1949.

7. Minutes of First Trial, p. 2288.

8. Allistair Cooke, *A Generation on Trial* (New York: Alfred A. Knopf, 1952), p. 164.

Chapter 3. The Case for the Defense

1. United States District Court for the Southern District of New York, *United States v. Alger Hiss*, Case No. C.128-402. June 1, 1949, Stenographer's Minutes, pp. 52–53.

2. Ibid., p. 53.

3. Allen Weinstein, *Perjury* (New York: Random House, 1997), p. 390.

4. Minutes of First Trial, *United States v. Alger Hiss*, "First Trial," (Wilmington, Del.: Scholarly Resources, Inc., June 22, 1949), p. 1611.

5. Sam Tanenhaus, *Whittaker Chambers* (New York: Random House, 1997), p. 387.

6. Ibid.

7. Minutes of First Trial, p. 2288.

8. Ibid., p. 2292.

9. Ibid., p. 2316.

10. Tanenhaus, p. 396.

11. Alistair Cooke, *A Generation on Trial* (New York: Alfred A. Knopf, 1952), p. 221.

12. Minutes of First Trial, p. 2475.

Chapter 4. The Summation

1. Sam Tanenhaus, *Whittaker Chambers* (New York: Random House, 1997), p. 400.

2. Minutes of First Trial, *United States v. Alger Hiss*, "First Trial," (Wilmington, Del.: Scholarly Resources, Inc., July 6, 1949), p. 2745–2756.

3. Ibid., p. 2843.

4. Ibid., p. 2856

5. Ibid., p. 2899.

6. Ibid., p. 2884.

7. Ibid., p. 2907.

8. Alistair Cooke, *A Generation on Trial* (New York: Alfred A. Knopf, 1952), pp. 264–265.

Chapter 5. The Case Goes to the Jury

1. Alistair Cooke, *A Generation on Trial* (New York: Alfred A. Knopf, 1952), p. 266.

2. Minutes of First Trial, *United States v. Alger Hiss*, "First Trial", (Wilmington, Del.: Scholarly Resources, Inc., July 7, 1949), p. 2930.

3. Ibid.

4. Cooke, p. 270.

5. Sam Tanenhaus, *Whittaker Chambers* (New York: Random House, 1997), p. 406.

6. Minutes of First Trial, p. 2962.

7. Tanenhaus, p. 411.

8. Cooke, p. 275.

Chapter 6. The Second Trial

1. Alger Hiss, *Recollections of a Life* (New York: Arcade Publishing, 1988), p. 214.

2. Ibid.

3. Whittaker Chambers, *Witness* (Washington, D.C.: Regnery Publishing, Inc., 1952), p. 791.

4. Hiss, p. 228.

5. Ibid., p. 381.

6. Allen Weinstein, *Perjury* (New York: Random House, 1997), p. 477.

7. Thomas Murphy's cross-examination of Dr. Carl A. Binger in *U.S. v. Alger Hiss* (Minnetonka, Minn.: The Professional Education Group, Inc., 1987), p. 44.

8. Weinstein, p. 432.

9. Ibid.

10. Thomas Murphy's Cross-examination, foreword.

11. Ibid., p. 95.

12. Ibid., p. 101.

13. Ibid., p. 102.

14. Ibid., pp. 101–102.

15. Ibid., p. 102.

16. Alger Hiss, *In the Court of Public Opinion* (New York: Alfred A. Knopf, 1957), p. 342.

17. Sam Tanenhaus, *Whittaker Chambers* (New York: Random House, 1997), p. 431.

18. Alistair Cooke, *A Generation on Trial* (New York: Alfred A. Knopf, 1952), p. 335.

19. Weinstein, p. 442.

20. Hiss, *In the Court of Public Opinion*, p. 323.

21. Minutes of Second Trial, *United States v. Alger Hiss*, "Second Trial," (Wilmington, Del.: Scholarly Resources, Inc., January 25, 1950), p. 3302.

22. Ibid., p. 3299.

23. Cooke, p. 338.

24. Hiss, *In the Court of Public Opinion*, p. 323.

25. Weinstein, p. 445.

26. Cooke, pp. 346–347.

27. Alger Hiss, *Recollections of a Life* (New York: Arcade Publishing, 1988), p. 228.

28. Tony Hiss, *The View From Alger's Window* (New York: Alfred A. Knopf, 1999), p. 227.

29. Cooke, p. 347.

30. Hiss, *In the Court of Public Opinion*, p. 401.

31. Ibid., pp. 413–414.

32. Ibid., p. 414.

33. Cooke, pp. 353–354.

34. Tanenhaus, p. 515.

Chapter 7. After the Verdict

1. Tony Hiss, *The View From Alger's Window* (New York: Alfred A. Knopf, 1999), p. 229.

2. Ibid.

3. Alger Hiss, *Recollections of a Life* (New York: Arcade Publishing, 1988), pp. 182–183.

4. Eric Breindel, "Hiss' Guilt: Goodies from the Venona Files," *The New Republic*, vol. 214, March 15, 1996, p. 18.

5. National Security Agency, "The Venona Documents," March 30, 1945, <www.nsa.gov/docs/venona/> (February 7, 2001).

6. Breindel, p. 18.

7. Eric Breindel, and Herbert Romerstein, "Hiss: Still Guilty," *The New Republic*, vol. 215, December 30, 1996, p. 12.

8. "Uncloaking the Soviet Spy Effort," *Wall Street Journal*, September 22, 1999, p. A22.

Glossary

appeal—To ask a court with greater authority to review the decision of a lower court.

bourgeoisie—The owners and managers of businesses in a capitalist society.

communism—A system of government that supports the ownership of all goods by all members of its society.

espionage—Spying; giving information to another country, knowing it will be used to harm the defense of the country it was taken from.

HUAC—House Un-American Activities Committee. This committee was formed to investigate people and organizations that were suspected of presenting a danger to American security. Also called the Dies Committee.

hypothetical question—A combination of assumed facts, representing a specific situation, on which an expert will be asked to state his opinion.

perjury—Lying under oath, either in court or in a sworn written statement. Perjury is a crime.

proletariat—The workers in a capitalist society.

prosecutor—An attorney who takes charge of the case against the accused in a trial, in the name of the government.

summation—Restating the most important points made during the trial, after all evidence has been presented. The attorneys for each side have an opportunity to sum up their arguments.

testimony—Evidence given by a witness under oath.

treason—The crime of trying to betray one's own country. A person can be convicted of treason only by confession in open court or by the testimony of two witnesses.

verdict—A decision made by a jury that has been chosen for the trial of a certain case.

Further Reading

Foster, Leila M. *The Story of the Cold War*. Danbury, Conn.: Children's Press, 1990.

Hiss, Tony. *The View From Alger's Window*. New York: Alfred A. Knopf, 1999.

Kort, Michael G. *The Cold War*. Brookfield, Conn.: Millbrook Press, Inc., 1994.

Rappoport, Doreen. *The Alger Hiss Trial*. New York: HarperCollins Children's Book Group, 1993.

Sherrow, Victoria. *Joseph McCarthy and the Cold War*. Woodbridge, Conn.: Blackbirch Press, Inc., 1998.

Tanenhaus, Sam. *Whittaker Chambers: A Biography*. New York: Random House, Inc., 1997.

Volkman, Ernest. *Spies: The Secret Agents Who Changed the Course of History*. New York: John Wiley and Sons, 1994.

Walker, Martin. *The Cold War*. New York: Henry Holt and Company, 1993.

Internet Addresses

FBI Freedom of Information Act—Venona

<http://foia.fbi.gov/venona.htm>

**National Archives and Records Administration—
Freedom of Information Act**

<http://www.nara.gov/foia>

National Security Agency—The Venona Project

<http://www.nsa.gov/docs/venona/>

Index

Pumpkin Papers, 48–49,
62–65, 67, 69, 70
Purge, 29

R

Reed, Justice Stanley, 68
Roosevelt, Eleanor, 60
Roosevelt, President Franklin
Delano, 33, 37

S

Sayre, Francis, 63
Stalin, Joseph, 16, 28–29, 31
State Department, 21
Stripling, Robert, 39, 60

Stryker, Lloyd Paul, 52, 58,
62, 65, 67, 70–71, 81–82
subversive people, 26

U

United Nations, 19–21

V

Venona Project, 107, 109

W

White, E. B., 26
Witt, Nathan, 37
Woodstock typewriter, 64–65,
67–68, 69, 75–76, 81, 83
World War II, 19, 33, 35
Wyzanski, Judge Charles, 68